Classic

LEGENDARY HERO STORIES

Other Classic Books by The Lyons Press

Classic & Antique Fly Fishing Tackle
Classic Adventure Stories
Classic American Locomotives
Classic Baseball Stories
Classic Cat Stories
Classic Christmas Stories
Classic Civil War Stories
Classic Climbing Stories
Classic Cowboy Stories
Classic Dog Stories
Classic Exploration Stories
Classic Fishing Stories
Classic Ghost Stories
Classic Golf Stories
Classic Horror Stories
Classic Horse Stories
Classic Hunting Stories
Classic Irish Stories
Classic New England Stories
Classic Love Stories
Classic Sailing Stories
Classic War Stories
Classic Survival Stories

Classic
LEGENDARY HERO STORIES

Extraordinary Tales of Honor, Courage, and Valor

EDITED *by*

STEPHEN VINCENT BRENNAN

THE LYONS PRESS
GUILFORD, CONNECTICUT
AN IMPRINT OF THE GLOBE PEQUOT PRESS

The Lyons Press is an imprint of
The Globe Pequot Press.

10   9   8   7   6   5   4   3   2   1

Printed in the United States of America

ISBN 1-59228-872-3

Library of Congress Cataloging-in-Publication Data
is available on file.

Contents

INTRODUCTION

IX

Rama
[R. C. DUTT]

1

Gilgamesh
[E. A. BUDGE]

15

Hercules
[THOMAS BULFINCH]

25

David
[FRANCES JENKINS OLCOTT]

35

Achilles
[HOMER]

43

Odysseus
[HOMER]

101

Beowulf
[JOHN EARLE]

123

Robin Hood
[HOWARD PYLE]   161

Tarzan
[EDGAR RICE BURROUGHS]   197

Zorro
[JOHNSTON MCCULLEY]   223

for the mighty Finn

Introduction

It is not for us to explain this flaming figure in terms of our tired and querulous culture. Rather we must try to explain ourselves by the blaze of such fixed stars.

—G. K. Chesterton
"The Maid of Orleans"

Did you bring along your telescope? No? Well, then, squint your eyes some, and tilt your head just so. There, you see it now? Just on the far horizon, or just above it. What is it? It looks like a smear or smudge, a stir of action certainly, an energy. It looks to be a kind of storm front, but perhaps it is only a swirling mist, a boiling fog from a long-ago time. Or is it a dust cloud raised by a troop of horse? Are the heavens parting? Is there to be a fresh deliverance, a new covenant, or just another hard rain? Perhaps it is some holocaust, tearing hot-footed in our direction? Then again, it may be Superman, come to save us. Whatever or whoever it is, it's coming from a long way off, and it's heading this way.

Once upon a time, a long time ago—or, as some native peoples say, not longer ago than yesterday—there rose up a Hero, a doer of mighty deeds and impossible tasks, a slayer of monsters, a savior of the people. Before long his name was in every mouth, his exploits noised abroad, his epics set in song, and whole sagas had grown up around him. These wondrous tales does the father teach his son, and he, his son and daughter, and they, their children, on and on down the ages. And every generation, in the retelling, recalls that first Hero, and to some extent, reshapes his story to best answer the preoccupations of its own time. Eventually some ink-spiller sets down his own version and the saga gels. But soon there are a hundred other written versions, adaptations and translations, and our Hero discovers himself the subject of poems, plays, ballets and operas. In our own age he is the subject of big movies and TV miniseries. It doesn't matter that he now bears only a little resemblance to that real, first, original Hero; because the plain facts of a person's life, his (or her) true autobiography, are not at issue here. He has long ago passed from history to legend.

But what accounts for the particular legends that have come down to us? Why one and not another? Our starry cosmology of history and of lore is full of the stories of men and women we don't much remember anymore. Many of them were truly "great" in their time. They built huge pyramids to their own memories, or chiseled their conquests in stone, or decked giant arc-like structures in the spoils of their triumphs. They may even still people our history books, and scholars may still squabble over their bones, their motivations, and chronologies, but they have never achieved legendary status.

How come some have made the cut and others have not? Luck plays a part in it; in the sense of a manuscript that is spared the rapine and pillage of the barbarian, or the fire in the library. The text of *Beowulf* comes to us from a single surviving eighth-century manuscript. We know of Gilgamesh because someone stumbled upon a hoard of clay tablets. It's a kind of miracle that we have many of these stories at all. If they had not survived, would other heroes have done just as well? Perhaps, but who would we substitute for the furious, swift-footed Achilles or the wily Odysseus? And doesn't our own idea of ourselves almost require that David trounce Goliath?

There's tradition as well; a legend involves a kind of wild democracy wherein the dead have a vote also. We remember these stories now because over time our ancestors *chose* to remember and remake and retell them. Strangely, it seems we are already committed to our Hero, already heavily invested in his saga, if for no other reason than we are collaborators in its remembering. Then again, the stories we tell our children are in a true sense our measure. So it is, and by this alchemy, we recognize that the legendary hero story is also our story, and he or she is us.

Put all this together and add one thing more—a true story. Not true in the narrow sense of historical fact, but rather a story that so embodies the sublime mysteries and commonplace terrors of life that we are moved to call it true. We say that we know the truth when we hear it, and we do. We also recognize that the title *Hero* is no mere honorific. For the legendary hero must live a hero's life, which means that he must partake of and participate in the tragedy and the comedy of life.

Hercules was the strongest man in the world, but he wasn't strong enough to control his strength. His intentions were good—his aim was to travel the world righting wrongs. His zeal in this ambition matched his strength, and this often got him in trouble with the gods, but he persevered in his attempts to do good—persevered to such a manic extent that he frequently went berserk and did much harm. Is this comedy or tragedy or both? Either way, we recognize the truth in it.

Rama, from the Indian epic *Ramayana*, translated *Rama's Way,* was determined to be the perfect prince, wise and compassionate, brave and strong, a trustworthy friend, a loving husband and brother, and an inspiring leader. He sought perfection in everything he did. But soon there were reverses at the palace and Rama went into exile, taking his brother and also his wife Sita, who was forthwith kidnapped and enslaved by the evil, lecherous, ten-headed King Ravana. Rama mounted the perfect rescue but it took some time. Shortly after they were reunited, Rama divorced Sita (though he loved her) because he could not be perfectly sure that she had been perfectly chaste during her long enslavement. This destroyed Sita (she was swallowed up by the earth) and blighted his life. Is this tragedy or is it divine comedy?

It does seem sometimes that much of life's a joke, or can be taken that way—or must be taken that way. You gotta laugh, you grin and bear it, you laugh through your tears. And laughter has always been a potent antidote to life's hardships, a relief from unbearable tension or grief, a strategy for coping. The leaven of humor—both high and low comedy—is a big part of the power of legend, and of our appreciation of it. In *Robin Hood,* we're treated to stories of heroes we know well; as told by Howard Pyle, they are downright comic. And why not? After all, Robin's adventures *were* "merry"— and so were his men.

Our last two selections, *Tarzan* and *Zorro*, are examples of very young legendary hero stories. *Tarzan* is only just over a hundred years old, and *Zorro* is even younger. It would be interesting, five hundred or a thousand years from now, to see how these upstarts have fared. Just now they suffer a little in comparison with the more ancient tales. They're not as rich generally, and these two legendary heroes tend to have things a little too much their own way. But it's early days. These are shortcomings typical of youth. For now we'll have to settle for them being merely great fun. So far as that goes, the other, older legendary hero stories, ain't got nothing on 'em.

—Stephen Vincent Brennan
Autumn, 2005

Rama

[R. C. DUTT]

Formerly there ruled over the kingdom of Kosala (capital Ayodhya) a king called Dasaratha. He belonged to the Solar race, and counted among his ancestors such famous names as Manu, Ikshvaku (first king of Ayodhya), Sagara, Bhagiratha (who brought the Ganges down from heaven), Kakutstha, and Raghu. He had three wives: Kausalya, Sumitra, and Kaikeyi; the first was the eldest, the last, the most beloved. Dasaratha ruled long and prosperously but had only one daughter, Santa and no sons, though he was getting old. Following the advice of Vasishtha, his family preceptor, Dasaratha offered a sacrifice in which his son-in-law Rishyasringa, officiated as head-priest. As a consequence, the king got four sons: 1. Rama, the eldest, born of Kausalya; 2. Bharata, born of Kaikeyi; 3. Lakshmana and 4. Satrughna, both born of Sumitra.

The kingdom of Videha (capital Mithila) was to the east of the kingdom of Kosala. It was at this time ruled by the saintly king Janaka, who, as he was once for a holy sacrifice preparing the ground with a plough, came upon an infant, and brought her up as his own daughter. This was Sita thus miraculously sprung from the Earth. The girl grew up in the company of Urmila, another daughter of Janaka, and of Mandavi and Srutakirti, daughters of Janaka's brother Kusadhwaja. As Sita became of an age to be married, Janaka instituted a *Sudvamvara*: whoever should succeed in bending a mighty bow (which Janaka had received from God Siva) was to marry the princess. Many attempted, but none succeeded.

One day there came to the court of Dasaratha the royal sage Visvamitra who, finding the demons frequently molesting his penances, requested the king to send two of his sons, Rama and Lakshmana, with him to his penance-grove. Since a person of Visvamitra's position could not be denied anything, Dasaratha reluctantly agreed to give over his sons, though yet in tender years. Visvamitra resumed his holy rites and when the molestors came, Rama, at Visvamitra's behest, killed the demon Subahu and the terrible she-demon Tataka. Pleased at the prince's valour, Visvamitra thereupon taught him the mystic formulae relating to all the missiles that he knew, and particularly the *Jrimbhaka* missile, which had the power of producing instantaneous stupor or paralysis in the ranks of the assailants. After the conclusion of the sacrifice, Visvamitra took Rama and Lakshmana with him to Mithila, the capital of Janaka. Janaka was very favourably impressed by the princes; and Visvamitra called upon Rama to try his hand at the mighty bow. Young though he was, Rama not only succeeded in bending it, but even breaking it in twain, and thus winning him a wife. Visvamitra now proposed that, along with Sita's marriage to Rama, there be celebrated the marriages of Sita's sister Urmila and her cousins Mandavi and Srutakirti to the three brothers of Rama, Lakshmana and Bharata and Satrughna respectively. The proposal was agreed to. Dasaratha was called from Ayodhya, and the marriages were celebrated with due pomp.

The nuptial joys, however, were interrupted by the arrival of Parasurama, son of Jamadagni. Parasurama was a fiery Brahman, sage and warrior, who had twenty-one times rid the earth of all Kshatriyas. He was a devotee of God Siva, and was incensed to learn that Rama had not only bent but broken the bow of his favourite Divinity. As nothing short of a fight with the young prince would satisfy him, Rama managed to reduce him to terms, and sent him away humbled and abashed. The four princes then returned to Ayodhya with their brides. Here they passed some twelve years. END OF BALAKANDA.

Dasaratha, finding his eldest son Rama now arrived at a proper age, resolves to crown him heir-apparent. Preparations are accordingly set on foot. But Kaikeyi, the youngest queen following the advice of Manthara, her nurse and confidante, calls upon her husband to fulfil immediately the two boons which on an earlier occasion he had granted her. Dasaratha consents, but is sorely grieved to learn that the boons are: 1. That Bharata, Kaikeyi's son, be appointed heir-apparent, 2. that Rama be forthwith sent away into exile for fourteen years. As the king could not belie his words, Rama had to submit to the wishes of his step-mother, which he cheerfully does. His wife Sita and his brother Lakshmana refuse to be left behind, and they are all three accordingly carried away through the weeping multitudes. The old king was so much afflicted by this great blow that he barely lived to hear the news of the exiles being taken over safe beyond the boundaries of his kingdom.

Bharata, who all this while was in utter ignorance of the happenings at Ayodhya, is now sent for in order to perform the obsequies of his father and assume the sovereignty thus devolved upon him. He returns; but discovering the mean conduct of his mother, he reproves her bitterly, and refuses to take charge of the kingdom and thus give his consent to the base intrigue. He resolves immediately to start in search of Rama, and to implore him to return. On the other side of the Ganges, near the mountain called Chitrakuta, close by the saint Bharadvaja's hermitage, Bharata finds Rama leading a forester's life in the company of his wife and brother. Rama is struck by Bharata's magnanimity, but insists upon the carrying out of his father's command to the letter, and is unwilling to return before the completion of the full term of fourteen years. Bharata thereupon resolves to keep company with Rama; the latter, however, reminds him of the duty they all owed to their subjects, and persuades him to return, which Bharata does, only on the condition that Rama will come back at the appointed time, himself in the meanwhile conducting the affairs of the state only as Rama's agent. END OF AYODHYA-KANDA.

Rama now resolves to withdraw further away from his kingdom and learning that the regions on the other side of the Vindhya mountains were infested with wild demons and cannibals, he set forth in that direction. At his entrance into the Vindhya forests he meets the demon Viradha, whom he kills. He then meets a number of sages and ascetics, in whose company he is said to have passed no less than ten years. Going further south into the Dandaka forests he reaches the river Godavari, and there, in the part of the country known as Janasthana, comes upon the hermitage of Agastya and his wife Lopamudra. The holy pair heartily welcome the newcomers, and here at the foot of a mountain called Prasravana, and in a region known as Panchavati, Rama resolves to build a small hut and to pass the rest of his exile peacefully in the company of the saint Agastya and the vulture-king Jatayus.

Peace, however, was not vouchsafed to him long. At this time there ruled in the island of Lanka (identified with modern Ceylon) a demon king, Ravana. He was called ten-headed and was a terror to the world. Having established his power in Lanka proper, Ravana crossed over to the mainland and overran the whole of Southern India, subduing everything that came in his way. Ravana, however, found more than his match in Valin, king of the Monkeys, whose kingdom comprised the part of South India then known as Kishkindha. An agreement was entered into whereby, except for a narrow strip of land along the coast, the bulk of the peninsula came into the possession of Valin. Ravana's territory touched the Janasthana, and here he left a large army of demons under the command of Khara (Ravana's younger brother) and Dushana and Trisiras.

Once Surpanakha, a widowed sister of Ravana, came upon Rama in the Panchavati, and smitten with his graceful form made him frank overtures of

love, promising to eat up Sita and thus put her out
of the way, if Rama would consent. Rama in jest
sent her to Lakshmana, who rewarded her insistence
by cutting off her nose and ears. Surpanakha went
weeping and bleeding to her brother Khara, who in
anger despatched fourteen picked men to capture
Rama. As they did not return, Khara marched with
his whole army, 14,000 demons strong and engaged
Rama in a close fight. Rama stepped back a few
paces so as to gain room for working with his bow,
and then, one after another, he killed the entire
army of demons, as also its three leaders.

Surpanakha vows revenge. She now repairs to
Ravana in Lanka and inflames his mind with a pas-
sion for Sita, whose charms she praises loudly.
Ravana resolves to capture her. He asks Maricha,
another demon, to assume the form of a golden
deer, and to lure Rama in chase away from his cottage. Maricha does this and is mortally wounded by
Rama's arrow. Before he dies, however, imitating the
voice of Rama, he calls upon Lakshmana for help.
Lakshmana was left behind to guard Sita in the cottage; but upon hearing the cry, which she mistook
for her husband's, Sita urges and even commands
Lakshmana to go, which he does reluctantly. Utilizing the favourable moment Ravana now pounces
upon the forlorn Sita and flies away with her, striking down on his way the vulture-king Jatayus, who

from his mountain peak had watched this daring act and attempted to intercept the abductor. Jatayus falls down to die, surviving just long enough to inform Rama and Lakshmana (already returned from the deer-chase amazed at not finding Sita in the cottage) of what had happened, Rama's grief was unbounded. END OF ARANYA-KANDA.

Wandering further onward, the princes at last reach the lake called Pampa. Here they come upon Sugriva and his trusty friend and minister Hanuman, alias Maruti. Sugriva was the brother of Valin, king of the Monkeys, and had been dispossessed by him both of his kingdom and his wife. Rama and Sugriva enter into an alliance whereby Rama agrees to restore Sugriva to his kingdom, and in return the latter promises to send out search-parties and help Rama to punish the abductor and recover his lost wife. Rama accordingly asks Sugriva to challenge Valin to a duel, and as the two brothers join in combat, Rama wounds Valin mortally with an arrow. For this unprovoked wrong and treachery Valin reproaches Rama severely; the latter simply replies that as an agent of the sovereign king of Ayodhya he took upon himself the duty of inflicting proper punishment upon malefactors who, like Valin had usurped a brother's throne and wife. The death of Valin leaves Sugriva master of the kingdom of Kishkindha; and in gratitude he now sends, under proper leaders, parties of Monkeys in search of

Sita. The most important of these was the one sent to the south under the command of Maruti. This party presses forward and southward until it gains the sea-coast. END OF KISHKINDHA-KANDA.

The waters seemed to offer an impassable barrier, as the island of Lanka stood on the other side of the ocean; but Maruti undertakes to clear it by a leap. This he does and enters Lanka. Here he was fortunate enough to meet Sita, sorrowing in Ravana's garden under the shade of an Asoka tree, she-demons of hideous and terrible looks keeping watch over her day and night. In glowing terms they describe to her the glory and the greatness of Ravana, and work alternately upon her hopes and her fears to the end that she may consent to have Ravana. Sita refuses to listen, and Ravana is too proud to stoop to force.

Maruti soon finds opportunity to console Sita and assure her of a speedy deliverance. Having thus achieved the chief object of his journey, Maruti now leaves Lanka, not without meeting sundry adventures, in the course of which he succeeds in killing a few hundred demons and setting the whole city on fire. Once more he leaps over the ocean and returns to Kishkindha with the glad news. END OF SUNDARAKANDA.

Rama immediately resolves to invade Lanka. Sugriva with his army of Monkeys and Jambavant with his army of Bears offer their assistance and the whole army soon gains the Southern Ocean. Here they are joined by Vibhishana, the youngest brother of Ravana. Vibhishana had tried to remonstrate with his eldest brother against the evil course of conduct he was pursuing, and being rewarded with contempt he now came over to Rama's side. Rama receives him well and promises him the kingdom of Lanka after Ravana's death. To make it possible for the army to cross over, Rama now resolves to construct a stone bridge over the ocean, and to this he is helped by the engineering genius of Nala. Having gained the island he next lays siege to the capital. The battle which follows lasts, according to the several inconsistent time-indications, for four or fifteen or thirty-nine or eighty-eight days; Ravana together with his brothers and sons and the entire army of demons is put to death; and Rama, in accordance with his promise, installs Vibhishana as king of Lanka.

Having thus vanquished the enemy and wiped out the insult, Rama now meets Sita. He is, however, unwilling, for fear of public scandal, to take his wife back until she has proved her purity. Pierced to the quick by Rama's suspicion Sita proposes the fire-ordeal. A huge pyre is kindled and with a firm tread she walks towards it and is engulfed by the flames. Immediately, however, she reappears, led forth by the Fire-god himself, who in the hearing of all proclaims her innocence. Rama now accepts her, saying that he never doubted her innocence, but had to do what he did for the sake of the people. The fourteen-year period of exile having now almost expired, Rama, along with his wife, brother, friends, and allies, makes a journey northwards, utilizing for the purpose the aerial car called *Pushpaka* which belonged to Ravana. They reach their home, where they meet Bharata and the Queen-mothers anxiously awaiting the return of the exiles, Rama's coronation is now celebrated with due pomp and there is rejoicing everywhere. END OF YUDDHA-KANDA.

The epic should naturally end here; but there is one more book or kanda dealing with the history of Rama from his coronation to his death. Here we are told how a few months after the coronation rumours regarding Sita began to be circulated amongst the people, who did not like that Rama should have received his wife back after she had been nearly a year in the house of Ravana. Through his spies Rama comes to know of this, and resolves to abandon Sita, although at this time she was in a state of advanced pregnancy. Rama charges his brother Lakshmana with the carrying out of this plan. Lakshmana obeys, places Sita in a chariot, takes her into a forest on the other side of the Ganges, and there leaves her, after communicating to her the actual state of things.

Thereupon Sita sends back to Rama a spirited reply and patiently succumbs to the inevitable. In her forlorn condition she fortunately chances upon the saint Valmiki, whose hermitage was near by. Valmiki receives the exiled queen under his protection. In his hermitage she gives birth to twin sons, Kusa and Lava, whom Valmiki brings up and educates along with his other pupils.

Meanwhile in Ayodhya Rama is not at peace. From a mere sense of duty he discharges his manifold functions as a king, but is always haunted by the image of her whom he had treated so unjustly. Years go by, and at last he resolves to perform a horse-sacrifice. For the festivities attending the completion of the sacrifice there came Valmiki bringing with him the twins, Kusa and Lava, whom he had taught to sing the Ramayana, a panegyric poem on Rama which Valmiki had composed. With great applause the boys recite the poem in the presence of Rama and the whole assembly. Rama inquires about the boys and is pleasantly surprised to learn from Valmiki that they are Rama's own sons. Understanding that Sita is still alive, he sends for her. Sita comes. Rama asks her to give further evidence of her innocence and purity. 'If it is true', exclaims Sita, 'that in mind and deed and word I have never been unfaithful to Rama, may Mother Earth receive me into her bosom!'. Just as she utters these words the Earth gapes open and a divine form stretches forth her hands to Sita, who enters the abyss and there finds eternal rest.

Soon after the disappearance of Sita, Rama feels his own end drawing near. The kingdom is divided amongst the four brothers, who in turn settle it upon their children. In the meantime the aged queen-mothers die. Thereafter Lakshmana whom Rama, for no fault of his own, was compelled to send away from him, gives up the ghost. Finally Rama himself enters the waters of the river Sarayu, and his other brothers, and the whole city of Ayodhya in fact, follow after him to heaven. END OF UTTARA-KANDA.

Gilgamesh

[E. A. BUDGE]

When the men who lived in the countries round about the head of the Persian Gulf, and along the rivers Euphrates and Tigris, first began to collect stories concerning this hero cannot be said, and we know nothing of the editors who gave them literary form. But it is quite certain that accounts of them written in Sumerian and Babylonian existed as early as 2000 B.C., and that, even at that remote period, many different versions of the deeds of Gilgamesh were in circulation. These facts indicate both the popularity and the antiquity of the Epic of Gilgamesh.

The stories about Gilgamesh were drawn up in a metrical form, and were probably learnt by heart by tribal singers who went from town to town, or from village to village, like the troubadours who lived

two or three thousand years later. Wherever warriors
went there went the name and fame of Gilgamesh.
And wherever the stories of his deeds went they
were heartily enjoyed, for every soldier loved, and
still loves, to hear of doughty deeds and hand-to-
hand fights. The Sumerians and Babylonians and
Assyrians were always fighting, sometimes each
other, sometimes the war-like natives of the hills to
the east and the north, and sometimes the ferocious
nomads in the desert to the west of the Euphrates.
In this way the fame of Gilgamesh reached the
mountains of Kurdistan and Armenia and the deserts
of the Jordan, and it no doubt penetrated the countries that we now call Syria and Palestine, and Egypt
and the coasts and islands of the Mediterranean.

The Epic filled a series of Twelve Tablets, and the
title given on the First Tablet is "He who has seen all
things." Gilgamesh was the fifth of a line of Sumerian kings who reigned at Erech, the modern Warka,
in Lower Babylonia; he is said to have reigned one
hundred and twenty-six years. He travelled in many
lands, and was all-wise and all-knowing, for two-
thirds of him were divine, and one-third was human.
Everywhere he did mighty deeds, a record of which
he had cut upon a stone tablet. He built the great
wall of Erech, and founded a temple; but he over-
worked his people, who were reduced to a state of
slavery, and they cried out to the gods to create a

rival to him, and to give them deliverance. The gods hearkened, and commanded the goddess Aruru to create Enkidu (Eabani), a being of unsurpassed stature and strength, whose body was covered with hair. This creature lived in the hills, ate herbs, and became lord of the forests. A hunter saw him one day in the forest and reported the fact to Gilgamesh, who sent the hunter back to the forest with a woman, whom he intended to ensnare Enkidu. When Enkidu saw her he straightway fell in love with her, and she persuaded him to return with her to Erech, and to forsake the company of the beasts of the forest. Enkidu went to Erech, and he and Gilgamesh became great friends. In Erech, Enkidu learnt to eat bread, drink beer, wear clothes, and use perfumes. He was a mighty hunter, and the people loved him, both for the spoils of the chase with which he supplied them abundantly, and also for his great courage. One day Gilgamesh arranged to go on a hunting expedition with him, but before they started they quarrelled about a woman. They appealed to arms, a fierce fight followed, and Enkidu was the victor, but the two warriors became greater friends than ever.

Soon after this Gilgamesh set out on an expedition against Khumbaba, a king of Elam, who lived in the mountains where the cedar trees grew, and took Enkidu with him. Khumbaba was keeper of the cedar trees, which were under the protection of Bel;

his breath was like a gale of wind, his voice was like the roar of a storm, and his mouth was like the mouth of the gods. Though terrified at the denseness of the forest Gilgamesh and Enkidu pressed on, and they slew Khumbaba, and returned in triumph to Erech. The goddess Ishtar noted their return, and sent for Gilgamesh and wanted him to become her lover, promising him every kind of luxury if he would consent. But he remembered the fate of all those who in times past had been cursed and slain through becoming her lover, and especially the sad end of Tammuz, the lover of her youth, who died a dreadful death. When Ishtar saw that her overtures were rejected she was filled with fury, and flying up to heaven, she told her father, Anu, and her mother, Antu, of the insults which Gilgamesh had heaped upon her. She called upon Anu to create a mighty bull to destroy him, and threatened to wreck the world if he would not grant her request. Anu created a monstrous, fire-breathing bull and sent it to Erech, where it killed many people. After a time Enkidu and Gilgamesh went out and killed the bull, whereupon Ishtar rushed out on the battlements of her temple in Erech and cursed Gilgamesh. All the people flocked to see the carcase of the beast, and they were amazed at the length of his horns. These Gilgamesh cut out and took to the temple of Lugalbanda, and hung them up on the throne of the god. As the heroes returned to the city the people crowded about them, and shouted praises to Gilgamesh.

Of the events that immediately followed these proceedings we know nothing, but it seems clear that Enkidu had a dream which portended calamity, and that soon afterwards he fell sick of some illness. He lay suffering on his bed for ten days, when his illness took a turn for the worse, and on the twelfth day he died. When Gilgamesh saw his friend lying still on his bed he thought that he was asleep, but when he found that he was really dead, his grief smote him so sorely that he roared like a lion and like a lioness robbed of her whelps. In bitter grief his mind went back to the days which he spent with his friend, "the panther of the desert," and to the joy of the chase, and to their joint slaughter of Khumbaba and Ishtar's bull; tears blinded his eyes and sobs choked his utterance. Turning from the dead body of Enkidu he set out for the open country and wandered about aimlessly, tortured the whole time with the agony of separation from his beloved "panther," and with the knowledge that his friend had not only left him but had left him for ever. Then, as the outbursts of grief became fewer and their intensity lessened, the awful thought dawned upon him that he must some day die like Enkidu, and like him become worthless dust! And the fear of death little by little drove grief from his mind, and he became filled with a passionate desire to escape from death. The more he thought about it, the more he was troubled, and then he remembered that his ancestor, Uta-Napishtim, the son of Ubara-Tutu, had become deified and so immortal. Forthwith he determined to seek out his ancestor and learn from him how to become immortal. Without delay he set out to go to the West, where Uta-Napishtim lived, and under the favour of Sin, the Moon-god, and Ishtar, the Queen of the gods, he marched all night. Soon after he started he was attacked by savage men or beasts, but he slew them and marched on to Mount Mashu, where the sun both rose and set. This mountain was guarded by terrible Scorpion-gods who slew men merely by looking at them. Quaking with fear, Gilgamesh did obeisance to them, and a Scorpion-goddess among them, recognising that two-thirds of Gilgamesh were god, caused him to be received with kindness into the mountain. Though his hosts told him that it was impossible for him to traverse that country, Gilgamesh pressed on and arrived twelve hours later in a lovely garden, which was filled with trees loaded with luscious fruits ripening under brilliant light.

Here in the region stood the palace of the goddess Siduri-Sabitu, and to it Gilgamesh went for help; the goddess, seeing him coming, had the gates closed. Eventually he had speech with the goddess, and he told her about the death of Enkidu, and his grief for him, and how he was now seeking his ancestor in order to learn how to escape from death. Finally he asked for information as to the road he should follow. The goddess Siduri-Sabitu told him that it was impossible for him to go where his ancestor was, because he could not cross the Waters of Death. Fortunately, Ur-Shanabi, the boatman of Uta-Napishtim, was in the place, and Gilgamesh went to him and, having made an agreement with him, reached the shore beyond the Waters of Death in one month and fifteen days. From his abode Uta-Napishtim watched the coming of his descendant, and he went down to the shore to meet him. Gilgamesh related the story of his travels and the reason for his coming, and Uta-Napishtim told him the Story of the Flood. As to his immediate quest, he told him also that no man can find out the day of his death, or escape from it. Utterly dissatisfied with this statement, which he refused to believe, Gilgamesh pressed Uta-Napishtim to give him further advice. In reply, the Immortal told him of a certain plant which grew at the bottom of the sea, and led him to believe that if he obtained possession of it he would become immortal. Gilgamesh set out with the boatman, and at a suitable place he tied stones to his feet and slid through the bottom of the boat down to the bottom of the sea, where he saw the plant growing. He plucked it and returned to the boat, and found that the plant was intended to make "the grey-headed old man to renew his youth."

Continuing his way back to Erech with the plant, Gilgamesh passed a pool of water which looked so cool and tempting that he dived into it and took a bath. Whilst he was disporting himself in the water, a serpent found, through its smell, the place where the plant was and ate it up. Sick and disgusted with this calamity, Gilgamesh sat down and wept and then in despair he turned his weary feet homeward to Erech. But the idea of escape from death obsessed him, and having failed to find the means of obtaining immortality upon earth, he determined to seek it in the Underworld. He consulted the priests on the subject, but the stipulations which they made were prohibitive, and he was obliged to give up the idea of going there himself. After much thought he came to the conclusion that if he could consult the spirit of his dead friend Enkidu, he might obtain some help from it. Thereupon he appealed to Bel to raise up the spirit of Enkidu, but the god answered not; he appealed to the Moon-god Sin with the same result. Next he cried to Ea for help, and this god ordered the warrior-god Nergal to produce the spirit of Enkidu, so that Gilgamesh might hold converse with it.

Then, Nergal having made an opening in the earth, the spirit of Enkidu appeared, and Gilgamesh asked him the question that was near his heart, but the spirit's answer was unsatisfactory, and Gilgamesh gained neither hope nor consolation from it. Thus he was forced to go on living and to face the fact that he must one day die and become even as Enkidu.

Hercules

[THOMAS BULFINCH]

Hercules (in Greek, Heracles) was the son of Jupiter and Alcmena. As Juno was always hostile to the offspring of her husband by mortal mothers, she declared war against Hercules from his birth. She sent two serpents to destroy him as he lay in his cradle, but the precocious infant strangled them with his own hands. He was however by the arts of Juno rendered subject to his cousin Eurystheus and compelled to perform all his commands. Eurystheus enjoined upon him a succession of desperate adventures, which are called the twelve "Labors of Hercules." The first was the fight with the Nemean lion. The valley of Nemea was infested by a terrible lion. Eurystheus ordered Hercules to bring him the skin of this monster. After using in vain his club and arrows against the lion, Hercules strangled the animal with his hands. He returned carrying the dead lion on his shoulders; but Eurystheus was so frightened at the sight of it and at this proof of the prodigious strength of the hero, that he ordered him to deliver the account of his exploits in future outside the town.

His next labor was to slaughter the Hydra. This monster ravaged the country of Argos, and dwelt in a swamp near the well of Amymone, of which the story is that when the country was suffering from drought, Neptune, who loved her, had permitted her to touch the rock with his trident, and a spring of three outlets burst forth. Here the Hydra took up his position, and Hercules was sent to destroy him. The Hydra had nine heads, of which the middle one was immortal. Hercules struck off its head with his club, but in the place of the head knocked off, two new ones grew forth each time. At length with the assistance of his faithful servant Iolaus, he burned away the heads of the Hydra, and buried the ninth or immortal one under a huge rock.

Another labor was the cleaning of the Augean stables. Augeas, king of Elis, had a herd of three thousand oxen, whose stalls had not been cleansed for thirty years. Hercules brought the rivers Alpheus and Peneus through them, and cleansed them thoroughly in one day.

His next labor was of a more delicate kind. Admeta, the daughter of Eurystheus, longed to obtain the girdle of the queen of the Amazons, and Eurystheus ordered Hercules to go and get it. The Amazons were a nation of women. They were very warlike and held several flourishing cities. It was their custom to bring up only the female children; the boys were either sent away to the neighboring nations or put to death. Hercules was accompanied by a number of volunteers, and after various adventures at last reached the country of the Amazons. Hippolyta, the queen, received him kindly, and consented to yield him her girdle; but Juno, taking the form of an Amazon, went among the other Amazons and persuaded them that the strangers were carrying off their queen. The Amazons instantly armed and came in great numbers down to the ship. Hercules, thinking that Hippolyta had acted treacherously, slew her, and taking her girdle, made sail homewards.

Another task enjoined him was to bring to Eurystheus the oxen of Geryon, a monster with three bodies, who dwelt in the island Erytheia (the red), so called because it lay at the west, under the rays of the setting sun. This description is thought to apply to Spain, of which Geryon was said to be king. After traversing various countries, Hercules reached at length the frontiers of Libya and Europe, where he raised the two mountains of Calpe and

Abyla, as monuments of his progress, or according to another account rent one mountain into two and left half on each side, forming the Straits of Gibraltar, the two mountains being called the Pillars of Hercules. The oxen were guarded by the giant Eurytion and his two-headed dog, but Hercules killed the giant and his dog and brought away the oxen in safety to Eurystheus.

The most difficult labor of all was bringing the golden apples of the Hesperides, for Hercules did not know where to find them. These were the apples which Juno had received at her wedding from the goddess of the Earth, and which she had entrusted to the keeping of the daughters of Hesperis, assisted by a watchful dragon. After various adventures Hercules arrived at Mount Atlas in Africa. Atlas was one of the Titans who had warred against the gods, and after they were subdued, Atlas was condemned to bear on his shoulders the weight of the heavens. He was the father of the Hesperides, and Hercules thought, might, if any one could, find the apples and bring them to him. But how to send Atlas away from his post, or bear up the heavens while he was gone? Hercules took the burden on his own shoulders, and sent Atlas to seek the apples. He returned with them, and though somewhat reluctantly, took his burden upon his shoulders again, and let Hercules return with the apples to Eurystheus.

Milton in his Comus makes the Hesperides the daughters of Hesperus, and nieces of Atlas:—

> —amidst the gardens fair
> Of Hesperus and his daughters three,
> That sing about the golden tree.

The poets, led by the analogy of the lovely appearance of the western sky at sunset, viewed the west as a region of brightness and glory. Hence they placed in it the Isles of the blest, the ruddy isle Erytheia, on which the bright oxen of Geryon were pastured, and the isle of the Hesperides. The apples are supposed by some to be the oranges of Spain, of which the Greeks had heard some obscure accounts.

A celebrated exploit of Hercules was his victory over Antæus. Antæus, the son of Terra (the Earth), was a mighty giant and wrestler, whose strength was invincible so long as he remained in contact with his mother Earth. He compelled all strangers who came to his country to wrestle with him, on condition that if conquered (as they all were), they should be put to death. Hercules encountered him, and finding that it was of no avail to throw him, for he always rose with renewed strength from every fall, he lifted him up from the earth and strangled him in the air.

Cacus was a huge giant, who inhabited a cave in Mount Aventine, and plundered the surrounding country. When Hercules was driving home the oxen of Geryon, Cacus stole part of the cattle, while the hero slept. That their foot-prints might not serve to show where they had been driven, he dragged them backward by their tails to his cave; so their tracks all seemed to show that they had gone in the opposite direction. Hercules was deceived by this stratagem, and would have failed to find his oxen, if it had not happened that in driving the remainder of the herd past the cave where the stolen ones were concealed, those within began to low, and were thus discovered. Cacus was slain by Hercules.

The last exploit we shall record was bringing Cerberus from the lower world. Hercules descended into Hades, accompanied by Mercury and Minerva. He obtained permission from Pluto to carry Cerberus to the upper air, provided he could do it without the use of weapons; and in spite of the monster's struggling he seized him, held him fast, and carried him to Eurystheus, and afterwards brought him back again. When he was in Hades he obtained the liberty of Theseus, his admirer and imitator, who had been detained a prisoner there for an unsuccessful attempt to carry off Proserpine.

Hercules in a fit of madness killed his friend Iphitus and was condemned for his offence to become the slave of Queen Omphale for three years. While in this service the hero's nature seemed changed. He lived effeminately, wearing at times the dress of a woman, and spinning wool with the handmaidens of Omphale, while the queen wore his lion's skin. When this service was ended, he married Dejanira and lived in peace with her three years. On one occasion as he was travelling with his wife, they came to a river, across which the Centaur Nessus carried travellers for a stated fee. Hercules himself forded the river, but gave Dejanira to Nessus to be carried across. Nessus attempted to run away with her, but Hercules heard her cries, and shot an arrow into the heart of Nessus. The dying Centaur told Dejanira to take a portion of his blood and keep it, as it might be used as a charm to preserve the love of her husband.

Dejanira did so, and before long fancied she had occasion to use it. Hercules in one of his conquests had taken prisoner a fair maiden, named Iole, of whom he seemed more fond than Dejanira approved. When Hercules was about to offer sacrifices to the gods in honor of his victory, he sent to his wife for a white robe to use on the occasion. Dejanira, thinking it a good opportunity to try her love-spell, steeped the garment in the blood of Nessus. We are to suppose she took care to wash out all traces of it, but the magic power remained, and as soon as the garment became warm on the body of Hercules, the poison penetrated into all his limbs and caused him the most intense agony. In his frenzy he seized Lichas, who had brought him the fatal robe, and hurled him into the sea. He wrenched off the garment, but it stuck to his flesh, and with it he tore away whole pieces of his body. In this state he embarked on board a ship and was conveyed home. Dejanira on seeing what she had unwittingly done, hung herself. Hercules, prepared to die, ascended Mount Œta, where he built a funeral pile of trees, gave his bow and arrows to Philoctetes, and laid himself down on the pile, his head resting on his club, and his lion's skin spread over him. With a countenance as serene as if he were taking his place at a festal board, he commanded Philoctetes to apply the torch. The flames spread apace and soon invested the whole mass.

Milton thus alludes to the frenzy of Hercules:—

As when Alides, from Œchalia crowned
With conquest, felt the envenomed robe, and tore,
Through pain, up by the roots Thessalian pines
And Lichas from the top of Œta threw
Into the Euboic Sea.

The gods themselves felt troubled at seeing the champion of the earth so brought to his end; but Jupiter with cheerful countenance thus addressed them: "I am pleased to see your concern, my princes, and am gratified to perceive that I am the ruler of a loyal people, and that my son enjoys your favor. For although your interest in him arises from his noble deeds, yet it is not the less gratifying to me. But now I say to you, Fear not. He who conquered all else is not to be conquered by those flames which you see blazing on Mount Œta. Only his mother's share in him can perish; what he derived from me is immortal. I shall take him, dead to earth, to the heavenly shores, and I require of you all to receive him kindly. If any of you feel grieved at his attaining this honor, yet no one can deny that he has deserved it." The gods all gave their assent; Juno only heard the closing words with some displeasure that she should be so particularly pointed at, yet not enough to make her regret the determination of her husband. So when the flames had consumed the mother's share of Hercules, the diviner part, instead of being injured thereby, seemed to start forth with new vigor, to assume a more lofty port and a more awful dignity. Jupiter enveloped him in a cloud, and took him up to a four-horse chariot to dwell among the stars. As he took his place in heaven, Atlas felt the added weight.

David

[FRANCES JENKINS OLCOTT]

Now there was a man of Benjamin, whose name was Kish, a mighty man of power. And he had a son, whose name was Saul, a choice young man, and a goodly. And there was not among the children of Israel a goodlier person than he. From his shoulders and upward he was higher than any of the people.

Then Samuel took a vial of oil, and poured it upon his head, and kissed him, and said, "Is it not because the Lord hath anointed thee to be captain over his inheritance?"

And Samuel said to all the people, "See ye him whom the Lord hath chosen, that there is none like him among all the people?" And all the people shouted, and said, "God save the king!"

Then Samuel told the people the manner of the kingdom, and wrote it in a book, and laid it up before the Lord. And Samuel sent all the people away, every man to his house.

Now the Philistines gathered together their armies to battle, and were gathered together at Shochoh, which belongeth to Judah, and pitched in Ephes-dammim. And Saul and the men of Israel were gathered together, and pitched by the valley of Elah, and set the battle in array against the Philistines. And the Philistines stood on a mountain on the one side, and Israel stood on a mountain on the other side: and there was a valley between them.

And there went out a champion out of the camp of the Philistines, named Goliath, of Gath, whose height was six cubits and a span. And he had an helmet of brass upon his head, and he was armed with a coat of mail; and the weight of the coat was five thousand shekels of brass. And he had greaves of brass upon his legs, and a target of brass between his shoulders. And the staff of his spear was like a weaver's beam; and his spear's head weighed six hundred shekels of iron. And one bearing a shield went before him.

And he stood and cried unto the armies of Israel, and said unto them, "Why are ye come out to set your battle in array? am not I a Philistine, and ye servants to Saul? choose you a man for you, and let him come down to me. If he be able to fight with me, and to kill me, then will we be your servants. But if I prevail against him, and kill him, then shall ye be our servants, and serve us." And the Philistine said, "I defy the armies of Israel this day. Give me a man, that we may fight together."

When Saul and all Israel heard those words of the Philistine, they were dismayed, and greatly afraid.

Now David was the son of that Ephrathite of Beth-lehem-judah, whose name was Jesse; and he had eight sons. And the man went among men for an old man in the days of Saul. And the three eldest sons of Jesse went and followed Saul to the battle. And David was the youngest: and the three eldest followed Saul. But David went and returned from Saul to feed his father's sheep at Beth-lehem.

And the Philistine drew near morning and evening, and presented himself forty days.

And Jesse said unto David his son, "Take now for thy brethren an ephah of this parched corn, and these ten loaves, and run to the camp to thy brethren. And carry these ten cheeses unto the captain of their thousand, and look how thy brethren fare, and take their pledge." Now Saul, and they, and all the men of Israel, were in the valley of Elah, fighting with the Philistines.

And David rose up early in the morning, and left the sheep with a keeper, and took, and went, as Jesse had commanded him. And he came to the trench, as the host was going forth to the fight, and shouted for the battle. For Israel and the Philistines had put the battle in array, army against army.

And David left his carriage in the hand of the keeper of the carriage, and ran into the army, and came and saluted his brethren. And as he talked with them, behold, there came up the champion, the Philistine of Gath, Goliath by name, out of the armies of the Philistines, and spake according to the same words: and David heard them.

And all the men of Israel, when they saw the man, fled from him, and were sore afraid. And the men of Israel said, "Have ye seen this man that is come up? surely to defy Israel is he come up. And it shall be, that the man who killeth him, the king will enrich him with great riches, and will give him his daughter, and make his father's house free in Israel."

And David spake to the men that stood by him, saying, "What shall be done to the man that killeth this Philistine, and taketh away the reproach from Israel? for who is this uncircumcised Philistine, that he should defy the armies of the living God?" And the people answered him after this manner, saying, "So shall it be done to the man that killeth him."

And Eliab his eldest brother heard when he spake unto the men; and Eliab's anger was kindled against David, and he said, "Why camest thou down hither? and with whom hast thou left those few sheep in the wilderness? I know thy pride, and the naughtiness of thine heart; for thou art come down that thou mightest see the battle."

And David said, "What have I now done? Is there not a cause?" And he turned from him toward another, and spake after the same manner: and the people answered him again after the former manner. And when the words were heard which David spake, they rehearsed them before Saul: and he sent for him.

And David said to Saul, "Let no man's heart fail because of him; thy servant will go and fight with this Philistine."

And Saul said to David, "Thou art not able to go against this Philistine to fight with him: for thou art but a youth, and he a man of war from his youth."

And David said unto Saul, "Thy servant kept his father's sheep, and there came a lion, and a bear, and took a lamb out of the flock. And I went out after him, and smote him, and delivered it out of his mouth. And when he arose against me, I caught him by his beard, and smote him, and slew him. Thy servant slew both the lion and the bear. And this uncircumcised Philistine shall be as one of them, seeing he hath defied the armies of the living God."

David said moreover, "The Lord that delivered me out of the paw of the lion, and out of the paw of the bear, he will deliver me out of the hand of this Philistine." And Saul said unto David, "Go, and the Lord be with thee."

And Saul armed David with his armour, and he put an helmet of brass upon his head; also he armed him with a coat of mail. And David girded his sword upon his armour, and he assayed to go; for he had not proved it. And David said unto Saul, "I cannot go with these; for I have not proved them." And David put them off him.

And he took his staff in his hand, and chose him five smooth stones out of the brook, and put them in a shepherd's bag which he had, even in a scrip; and his sling was in his hand. And he drew near to the Philistine.

And the Philistine came on and drew near unto David; and the man that bare the shield went before him. And when the Philistine looked about, and saw David, he disdained him: for he was but a youth, and ruddy, and of a fair countenance. And the Philistine said unto David, "Am I a dog, that thou comest to me with staves?" And the Philistine cursed David by his gods. And the Philistine said to David, "Come to me, and I will give thy flesh unto the fowls of the air, and to the beasts of the field."

Then said David to the Philistine, "Thou comest to me with a sword, and with a spear, and with a shield; but I come to thee in the name of the Lord of hosts, the God of the armies of Israel, whom thou hast defied. This day will the Lord deliver thee into mine hand; and I will smite thee, and take thine head from thee; and I will give the carcases of the host of the Philistines this day unto the fowls of the air, and to the wild beasts of the earth; that all the earth may know that there is a God in Israel. And all this assembly shall know that the Lord saveth not with sword and spear: for the battle is the Lord's, and he will give you into our hands."

And it came to pass, when the Philistine arose, and came and drew nigh to meet David, that David hasted, and ran toward the army to meet the Philistine. And David put his hand in his bag, and took thence a stone, and slang it, and smote the Philistine in his forehead, that the stone sunk into his forehead; and he fell upon his face to the earth.

So David prevailed over the Philistine with a sling and with a stone, and smote the Philistine, and slew him; but there was no sword in the hand of David. Therefore David ran, and stood upon the Philistine, and took his sword, and drew it out of the sheath thereof, and slew him, and cut off his head therewith. And when the Philistines saw their champion was dead, they fled.

And the men of Israel and of Judah arose, and shouted, and pursued the Philistines, until thou come to the valley, and to the gates of Ekron. And the wounded of the Philistines fell down by the way. And the children of Israel returned from chasing after the Philistines, and they spoiled their tents.

And David took the head of the Philistine, and brought it to Jerusalem; but he put his armour in his tent.

Achilles

[HOMER]

THE ILIAD BOOK XIX

Now when Dawn in robe of saffron was hasting from the streams of Oceanus, to bring light to mortals and immortals, Thetis reached the ships with the armour that the god had given her. She found her son fallen about the body of Patroclus and weeping bitterly. Many also of his followers were weeping round him, but when the goddess came among them she clasped his hand in her own, saying, "My son, grieve as we may we must let this man lie, for it is by heaven's will that he has fallen; now, therefore, accept from Vulcan this rich and goodly armour, which no man has ever yet borne upon his shoulders."

As she spoke she set the armour before Achilles, and it rang out bravely as she did so. The Myrmidons were struck with awe, and none dared look full at it, for they were afraid; but Achilles was roused to still greater fury, and his eyes gleamed with a fierce light, for he was glad when he handled the splendid present which the god had made him. Then, as soon as he had satisfied himself with looking at it, he said to his mother, "Mother, the god has given me armour, meet handiwork for an immortal and such as no man living could have fashioned; I will now arm, but I much fear that flies will settle upon the son of Menœtius and breed worms about his wounds, so that his body, now he is dead, will be disfigured and the flesh will rot."

Silver-footed Thetis answered, "My son, be not disquieted about this matter. I will find means to protect him from the swarms of noisome flies that prey on the bodies of men who have been killed in battle. He may lie for a whole year, and his flesh shall still be as sound as ever, or even sounder. Call, therefore, the Achæan heroes in assembly; unsay your anger against Agamemnon; arm at once, and fight with might and main."

As she spoke she put strength and courage into his heart, and she then dropped ambrosia and red nectar into the wounds of Patroclus, that his body might suffer no change.

Then Achilles went out upon the sea-shore, and with a loud cry called on the Achæan heroes. On this even those who as yet had stayed always at the ships, the pilots and helmsmen, and even the stewards who were about the ships and served out rations, all came to the place of assembly because Achilles had shown himself after having held aloof so long from fighting. Two sons of Mars, Ulysses and the son of Tydeus, came limping, for their wounds still pained them; nevertheless they came, and took their seats in the front row of the assembly. Last of all came Agamemnon, king of men, he too wounded, for Coön son of Antenor had struck him with a spear in battle.

When the Achæans were got together Achilles rose and said, "Son of Atreus, surely it would have been better alike for both you and me, when we two were in such high anger about Briseis, surely it would have been better, had Diana's arrow slain her at the ships on the day when I took her after having sacked Lyrnessus. For so, many an Achæan the less would have bitten dust before the foe in the days of my anger. It has been well for Hector and the Trojans, but the Achæans will long indeed remember our quarrel. Now, however, let it be, for it is over. If we have been angry, necessity has schooled our anger. I put it from me: I dare not nurse it for ever; therefore, bid the Achæans arm forthwith that I may go out against the Trojans, and learn whether they will be in a mind to sleep by the ships or no. Glad, I ween, will he be to rest his knees who may fly my spear when I wield it."

Thus did he speak, and the Achæans rejoiced in that he had put away his anger.

Then Agamemnon spoke, rising in his place, and not going into the middle of the assembly. "Danaan heroes," said he, "servants of Mars, it is well to listen when a man stands up to speak, and it is not seemly to interrupt him, or it will go hard even with a practiced speaker. Who can either hear or speak in an uproar? Even the finest orator will be disconcerted by it. I will expound to the son of Peleus, and do you other Achæans heed me and mark me well. Often have the Achæans spoken to me of this matter and upbraided me, but it was not I that did it: Jove, and Fate, and Erinys that walks in darkness struck me mad when we were assembled on the day that I took from Achilles the meed that had been awarded to him. What could I do? All things are in the hand of heaven, and Folly, eldest of Jove's daughters, shuts men's eyes to their destruction. She walks delicately, not on the solid earth, but hovers over the heads of men to make them stumble or to ensnare them.

"Time was when she fooled Jove himself, who they say is greatest whether of gods or men; for Juno, woman though she was, beguiled him on the day when Alcmena was to bring forth mighty Hercules in the fair city of Thebes. He told it out among the gods saying, 'Hear me all gods and goddesses, that I may speak even as I am minded; this day shall an Ilithuia, helper of women who are in labour, bring a man child into the world who shall be lord over all that dwell about him who are of my blood and lineage.' Then said Juno all crafty and full of guile, 'You will play false, and will not hold to your word. Swear me, O Olympian, swear me a great oath, that he who shall this day fall between the feet of a woman, shall be lord over all that dwell about him who are of your blood and lineage.'

"Thus she spoke, and Jove suspected her not, but swore the great oath, to his much ruing thereafter. For Juno darted down from the high summit of Olympus, and went in haste to Achæan Argos where she knew that the noble wife of Sthenelus son of Perseus then was. She being with child and in her seventh month, Juno brought the child to birth though there was a month still wanting, but she stayed the offspring of Alcmena, and kept back the Ilithuiæ. Then she went to tell Jove the son of Saturn, and said, 'Father Jove, lord of the lightning—I have a word for your ear. There is a fine child born this day, Eurystheus, son to Sthenelus the son of Perseus; he is of your lineage; it is well, therefore, that he should reign over the Argives.'

"On this Jove was stung to the very quick, and in his rage he caught Folly by the hair, and swore a great oath that never should she again invade starry heaven and Olympus, for she was the bane of all.

Then he whirled her round with a twist of his hand, and flung her down from heaven so that she fell on to the fields of mortal men; and he was ever angry with her when he saw his son groaning under the cruel labors that Eurystheus laid upon him. Even so did I grieve when mighty Hector was killing the Argives at their ships, and all the time I kept thinking of Folly who had so baned me. I was blind, and Jove robbed me of my reason; I will now make atonement, and will add much treasure by way of amends. Go, therefore, into battle, you and your people with you. I will give you all that Ulysses offered you yesterday in your tents: or if it so please you, wait, though you would fain fight at once, and my squires shall bring the gifts from my ship, that you may see whether what I give you is enough."

And Achilles answered, "Son of Atreus, king of men Agamemnon, you can give such gifts as you think proper, or you can withhold them: it is in your own hands. Let us now set battle in array; it is not well to tarry talking about trifles, for there is a deed which is as yet to do. Achilles shall again be seen fighting among the foremost, and laying low the ranks of the Trojans: bear this in mind each one of you when he is fighting."

Then Ulysses said, "Achilles, godlike and brave, send not the Achæans thus against Ilius to fight the Trojans fasting, for the battle will be no brief one, when it is once begun, and heaven has filled both sides with fury; bid them first take food both bread and wine by the ships, for in this there is strength and stay. No man can do battle the livelong day to the going down of the sun if he is without food; however much he may want to fight his strength will fail him before he knows it; hunger and thirst will find him out, and his limbs will grow weary under him. But a man can fight all day if he is full fed with meat and wine; his heart beats high, and his strength will stay till he has routed all his foes; there-fore, send the people away and bid them prepare their meal; King Agamemnon will bring out the gifts in presence of the assembly, that all may see them and you may be satisfied. Moreover let him swear an oath before the Argives that he has never gone up into the couch of Briseis, nor been with her after the manner of men and women; and do you, too, show yourself of a gracious mind; let Agamemnon entertain you in his tents with a feast of reconciliation, that so you may have had your dues in full. As for you, son of Atreus, treat people more righteously in future; it is no disgrace even to a king that he should make amends if he was wrong in the first instance."

And King Agamemnon answered, "Son of Laertes, your words please me well, for throughout you have spoken wisely. I will swear as you would have me do; I do so of my own free will, neither shall I take the name of heaven in vain. Let, then, Achilles wait, though he would fain fight at once, and do you others wait also, till the gifts come from my tent and we ratify the oath with sacrifice. Thus, then, do I charge you: take some noble young Achæans with you, and bring from my tents the gifts that I promised yesterday to Achilles, and bring the women also; furthermore let Talthybius find me a boar from those that are with the host, and make it ready for sacrifice to Jove and to the sun."

Then said Achilles, "Son of Atreus, king of men Agamemnon, see to these matters at some other season, when there is breathing time and when I am calmer. Would you have men eat while the bodies of those whom Hector son of Priam slew are still lying mangled upon the plain? Let the sons of the Achæans, say I, fight fasting and without food, till we have avenged them; afterwards at the going down of the sun let them eat their fill. As for me, Patroclus is lying dead in my tent, all hacked and hewn, with his feet to the door, and his comrades are mourning round him. Therefore I can take thought of nothing save only slaughter and blood and the rattle in the throat of the dying."

Ulysses answered, "Achilles, son of Peleus, mightiest of all the Achæans, in battle you are better than I, and that more than a little, but in counsel I am much before you, for I am older and of greater knowledge. Therefore be patient under my words. Fighting is a thing of which men soon surfeit, and when Jove, who is war's steward, weighs the upshot, it may well prove that the straw which our sickles have reaped is far heavier than the grain. It may not be that the Achæans should mourn the dead with their bellies; day by day men fall thick and threefold continually; when should we have respite from our sorrow? Let us mourn our dead for a day and bury them out of sight and mind, but let those of us who are left eat and drink that we may arm and fight our foes more fiercely. In that hour let no man hold back, waiting for a second summons; such summons shall bode ill for him who is found lagging behind at our ships; let us rather sally as one man and loose the fury of war upon the Trojans."

When he had thus spoken he took with him the sons of Nestor, with Meges son of Phyleus, Thoas, Meriones, Lycomedes son of Creontes, and Mela-nippus, and went to the tent of Agamemnon son of Atreus. The word was not sooner said than the deed was done: they brought out the seven tripods which Agamemnon had promised, with the twenty metal cauldrons and the twelve horses; they also brought the women skilled in useful arts, seven in number, with Briseis, which made eight. Ulysses weighed out the ten talents of gold and then led

the way back, while the young Achæans brought
the rest of the gifts, and laid them in the middle of
the assembly.

Agamemnon then rose, and Talthybius whose
voice was like that of a god came up to him with the
boar. The son of Atreus drew the knife which he
wore by the scabbard of his mighty sword, and began
by cutting off some bristles from the boar, lifting up
his hands in prayer as he did so. The other Achæans
sat where they were all silent and orderly to hear the
king, and Agamemnon looked into the vault of
heaven and prayed saying, "I call Jove the first and
mightiest of all gods to witness, I call also Earth and
Sun and the Erinyes who dwell below and take
vengeance on him who shall swear falsely, that I have
laid no hand upon the girl Briseis, neither to take her
to my bed nor otherwise, but that she has remained
in my tents inviolate. If I swear falsely may heaven
visit me with all the penalties which it metes out to
those who perjure themselves."

He cut the boar's throat as he spoke, whereon
Talthybius whirled it round his head, and flung it
into the wide sea to feed the fishes. Then Achilles
also rose and said to the Argives, "Father Jove, of a
truth you blind men's eyes and bane them. The son
of Atreus had not else stirred me to so fierce and
anger, nor so stubbornly taken Briseis from me
against my will. Surely Jove must have counselled

the destruction of many an Argive. Go, now, and take your food that we may begin fighting."

On this he broke up the assembly, and every man went back to his own ship. The Myrmidons attended to the presents and took them away to the ship of Achilles. They placed them in his tents, while the stable-men drove the horses in among the others.

Briseis, fair as Venus, when she saw the mangled body of Patroclus, flung herself upon it and cried aloud, tearing her breast, her neck, and her lovely face with both her hands. Beautiful as a goddess she wept and said, "Patroclus, dearest friend, when I went hence I left you living; I return, O prince, to find you dead; thus do fresh sorrows multiply upon me one after the other. I saw him to whom my father and mother married me, cut down before our city, and my three own dear brothers perished with him on the self-same day; but you, Patroclus, even when Achilles slew my husband and sacked the city of noble Mynes, told me that I was not to weep, for you said you would make Achilles marry me, and take me back with him to Phthia, where we should have a wedding feast among the Myrmidons. You were always kind to me and I shall never cease to grieve for you."

She wept as she spoke, and the women joined in her lament—making as though their tears were for Patroclus, but in truth each was weeping for her own sorrows. The elders of the Achæans gathered round Achilles and prayed him to take food, but he groaned and would not do so. "I pray you," said he, "if any comrade will hear me, bid me neither eat nor drink, for I am in great heaviness, and will stay fasting even to the going down of the sun."

On this he sent the other princes away, save only the two sons of Atreus and Ulysses, Nestor, Idomeneus, and the old knight Phœnix, who stayed behind and tried to comfort him in the bitterness of his sorrow: but he would not be comforted till he should have flung himself into the jaws of battle, and he fetched sigh on sigh, thinking ever of Patroclus. Then he said—

"Hapless and dearest comrade, you it was who would get a good dinner ready for me at once and without delay when the Achæans were hasting to fight the Trojans; now, therefore, though I have meat and drink in my tents, yet will I fast for sorrow. Grief greater than this I could not know, not even though I were to hear of the death of my father, who is now in Phthia weeping for the loss of me his son, who am here fighting the Trojans in a strange land for the accursed sake of Helen, nor yet though I should hear that my son is no more—he who is being brought up in Seyros—if indeed Neoptolemus is still living. Till now I made sure that I alone was to fall here at Troy away from Argos, while you

were to return to Phthia, bring back my son with
you in your own ship, and show him all my property,
my bondsmen, and the greatness of my house—for
Peleus must surely be either dead, or what little life
remains to him is oppressed alike with the infirmi-
ties of age and ever present fear lest he should hear
the sad tidings of my dead."

He wept as he spoke, and the elders sighed in
concert as each thought on what he had left at
home behind him. The son of Saturn looked down
with pity upon them, and said presently to Minerva,
"My child, you have quite deserted your hero; is he
then gone so clean out of your recollection? There
he sits by the ships all desolate for the loss of his dear
comrade, and though the others are gone to their
dinner he will neither eat nor drink. Go then and
drop nectar and ambrosia into his breast, that he
may know no hunger."

With these words he urged Minerva, who was already of the same mind. She darted down from
heaven into the air like some falcon sailing on his
broad wings and screaming. Meanwhile the Achæans
were arming throughout the host, and when Minerva had dropped nectar and ambrosia into Achilles
so that no cruel hunger should cause his limbs to fail
him, she went back to the house of her mighty father. Thick as the chill snow-flakes shed from the
hand of Jove and borne on the keen blasts of the

north wind, even so thick did the gleaming helmets, the bossed shields, the strongly plated breastplates, and the ashen spears stream from the ships. The sheen pierced the sky, the whole land was radiant with their flashing armour, and the sound of the tramp of their treading rose from under their feet. In the midst of them all Achilles put on his armour; he gnashed his teeth, his eyes gleamed like fire, for his grief was greater than he could bear. Thus, then, full of fury against the Trojans, did he don the gift of the god, the armour that Vulcan had made him.

First he put on the goodly greaves fitted with ancle-clasps, and next he did on the breastplate about his chest. He slung the silver-studded sword of bronze about his shoulders, and then took up the shield so great and strong that shone afar with a splendour as of the moon. As the light seen by sailors from out at sea, when men have lit a fire in their homestead high up among the mountains, but the sailors are carried out to sea by wind and storm far from the haven where they would be—even so did the gleam of Achilles' wondrous shield strike up into the heavens. He lifted the redoubtable helmet, and set it upon his head, from whence it shone like a star, and the golden plumes which Vulcan had set thick about the ridge of the helmet, waved all around it. Then Achilles made trial of himself in his armour to see whether it fitted him, so that his limbs could play freely under it, and it seemed to buoy him up as though it had been wings.

He also drew his father's spear out of the spear-stand, a spear so great and heavy and strong that none of the Achæans save only Achilles had strength to wield it; this was the spear of Pelian ash from the topmost ridges of Mt. Pelion, which Chiron had once given to Peleus, fraught with the death of heroes. Automedon and Alcimus busied themselves with the harnessing of his horses; they made the bands fast about them, and put the bit in their mouths, drawing the reins back towards the chariot. Automedon, whip in hand, sprang up behind the horses, and after him Achilles mounted in full armour, resplendent as the sun-god Hyperion. Then with a loud voice he chided with his father's horses saying, "Xanthus and Balius, famed offspring of Podarge—this time when we have done fighting be sure and bring your driver safely back to the host of the Achæans, and do not leave him dead on the plain as you did Patroclus."

Then fleet Xanthus answered from under the yoke—for white-armed Juno had endowed him with human speech—and he bowed his head till his mane touched the ground as it hung down from under the yoke-band. "Dread Achilles," said he, "we will indeed save you now, but the day of your death is near, and the blame will not be ours, for it will be heaven and stern fate that will destroy you. Neither was it through any sloth or slackness on our part that the Trojans stripped Patroclus of his armour; it was the mighty god whom lovely Leto bore that slew him as he fought among the foremost, and vouchsafed a triumph to Hector. We two can fly as swiftly as Zephyrus who they say is fleetest of all winds; nevertheless it is your doom to fall by the hand of a man and of a god."

When he had thus said the Erinyes stayed his speech, and Achilles answered him in great sadness, saying, "Why, O Xanthus, do you thus foretell my death? You need not do so, for I well know that I am to fall here, far from my dear father and mother; none the more, however, shall I stay my hand till I have given the Trojans their fill of fighting."

So saying, with a loud cry he drove his horses to the front.

BOOK XX

Thus, then, did the Achæans arm by their ships round you, O son of Peleus, who were hungering for battle; while the Trojans over against them armed upon the rise of the plain.

Meanwhile Jove from the top of many-delled Olympus, bade Themis gather the gods in council, whereon she went about and called them to the house of Jove. There was not a river absent except Oceanus, nor a single one of the nymphs that haunt fair groves, or springs of rivers and meadows of green grass. When they reached the house of cloud-compelling Jove, they took their seats in the arcades of polished marble which Vulcan with his consummate skill had made for father Jove.

In such wise, therefore, did they gather in the house of Jove. Neptune also, lord of the earthquake, obeyed the call of the goddess, and came up out of the sea to join them. There, sitting in the midst of them, he asked what Jove's purpose might be. "Why," said he, "wielder of the lightning, have you called the gods in council? Are you considering some matter that concerns the Trojans and Achæans—for the blaze of battle is on the point of being kindled between them?"

And Jove answered, "You know my purpose, shaker of earth, and wherefore I have called you hither. I take thought for them even in their destruction. For my own part I shall stay here seated on Mt. Olympus and look on in peace, but do you others go about among the Trojans and Achæans, and help either side as you may be severally disposed. If Achilles fights the Trojans without hindrance they will made no stand against him; they have ever trembled at the sight of him, and now that he is roused to such fury about his comrade, he will override fate itself and storm their city."

Thus spoke Jove and gave the word for war, whereon the gods took their several sides and went into battle. Juno, Pallas Minerva, earth-encircling Neptune, Mercury bringer of good luck and excellent in all cunning—all these joined the host that came from the ships; with them also came Vulcan in all his glory, limping, but yet with his thin legs plying lustily under him. Mars of gleaming helmet joined the Trojans, and with him Apollo of locks unshorn, and the archer goddess Diana, Leto, Xanthus, and laughter-loving Venus.

So long as the gods held themselves aloof from mortal warriors the Achæans were triumphant, for Achilles who had long refused to fight was now with them. There was not a Trojan but his limbs failed him for fear as he beheld the fleet son of Peleus all glorious in his armour, and looking like Mars himself. When, however, the Olympians came to take their part among men, forthwith uprose strong Strife, rouser of hosts, and Minerva raised her loud voice, now standing by the deep trench that ran outside the wall, and now shouting with all her might upon the shore of the sounding sea. Mars also bellowed out upon the other side, dark as some black thunder-cloud, and called on the Trojans at the top of his voice, now from the acropolis, and now speeding up the side of the river Simois till he came to the hill Callicolone.

Thus did the gods spur on both hosts to fight, and rouse fierce contention also among themselves. The sire of gods and men thundered from heaven above, while from beneath Neptune shook the vast earth, and bade the high hills tremble. The spurs and crests of many-fountained Ida quaked, as also the city of the Trojans and the ships of the Achæans. Hades, king of the realms below, was struck with fear; he sprang panic-stricken from his throne and cried aloud in terror lest Neptune, lord of the earthquake, should crack the ground over his head, and lay bare his mouldy mansions to the sight of mortals and im- mortals—mansions so ghastly grim that even the gods shudder to think of them. Such was the uproar as the gods came together in battle. Apollo with his arrows took his stand to face King Neptune, while Minerva took hers against the god of war; the archer-goddess Diana with her golden arrows, sister of far-darting Apollo, stood to face Juno; Mercury the lusty bringer of good luck faced Leto, while the mighty eddying river whom men call Scamander, but gods Xanthus, matched himself against Vulcan.

The gods, then, were thus ranged against one an- other. But the heart of Achilles was set on meeting Hector son of Priam, for it was with his blood that he longed above all things else to glut the stubborn lord of battle. Meanwhile Apollo set Æneas on to attack the son of Peleus, and put courage into his heart, speaking with the voice of Lycaon son of Priam. In his likeness, therefore, he said to Æneas, "Æneas, counselor of the Trojans, where are now the brave words with which you vaunted over your wine before the Trojan princes, saying that you would fight Achilles son of Peleus in single combat?"

And Æneas answered, "Why do you thus bid me fight the proud son of Peleus, when I am in no mind to do so? Were I to face him now, it would not be for the first time. His spear has already put me to fight from Ida, when he attacked our cattle and sacked Lyrnessus and Pedasus; Jove indeed saved me in that he vouchsafed me strength to fly, else had I fallen by the hands of Achilles and Minerva, who went before him to protect him and urged him to fall upon the Lelegæ and Trojans. No man may fight Achilles, for one of the gods is always with him as his guardian angel, and even were it not so, his weapon flies ever straight, and fails not to pierce the flesh of him who is against him; if heaven would let me fight him on even terms he should not soon overcome me, though he boasts that he is made of bronze."

Then said King Apollo, son to Jove, "Nay, hero, pray to the ever-living gods, for men say that you were born of Jove's daughter Venus, whereas Achilles is son to a goddess of inferior rank. Venus is child to Jove, while Thetis is but daughter to the old man of the sea. Bring, therefore, your spear to bear upon him, and let him not scare you with his taunts and menaces."

As he spoke he put courage into the heart of the shepherd of his people, and he strode in full armour among the ranks of the foremost fighters. Nor did the son of Anchises escape the notice of white-armed Juno, as he went forth into the throng to meet Achilles. She called the gods about her, and said, "Look to it, you two, Neptune and Minerva, and consider how this shall be; Phœbus Apollo has been sending Æneas clad in full armor to fight Achilles. Shall we turn him back at once, or shall one of us stand by Achilles and endow him with strength so that his heart fail not, and he may learn that the chiefs of the immortals are on his side, while the others who have all along been defending the Trojans are but vain helpers? Let us all come down from Olympus and join in the fight, that this day he may take no hurt at the hands of the Trojans. Hereafter let him suffer whatever fate may have spun out for him when he was begotten and his mother bore him. If Achilles be not thus assured by the voice of a god, he may come to fear presently when one of us meets him in battle, for the gods are terrible if they are seen face to face."

Neptune lord of the earthquake answered her saying, "Juno, restrain your fury; it is not well; I am not in favour of forcing the other gods to fight us,

for the advantage is too greatly on our own side;
let us take our places on some hill out of the
beaten track, and let mortals fight it out among
themselves. If Mars Phœbus Apollo begin fighting,
or keep Achilles in check so that he cannot fight,
we, too, will at once raise the cry of battle, and in
that case they will soon leave the field and go back
vanquished to Olympus among the other gods."

With these words the dark-haired god led the
way to the high earth-barrow of Hercules, built
round solid masonry, and made by the Trojans
and Pallas Minerva for him to fly to when the sea-
monster was chasing him from the shore on to the
plain. Here Neptune and those that were with him
took their seats, wrapped in a thick cloud of darkness; but the other gods seated themselves on the
brow of Callicolone round you, O Phœbus, and
Mars the waster of cities.

Thus did the gods sit apart and form their plans,
but neither side was willing to begin battle with the
other, and Jove from his seat on high was in command over them all. Meanwhile the whole plain was
alive with men and horses, and blazing with the
gleam of armour. The earth rang again under the
tramp of their feet as they rushed towards each
other, and two champions, by far the foremost of
them all, met between the hosts to fights—to wit,
Æneas son of Anchises, and noble Achilles.

Æneas was first to stride forward in attack, his doughty helmet tossing defiance as he came on. He held his strong shield before his breast, and brandished his bronze spear. The son of Peleus from the other side sprang forth to meet him, like some fierce lion that the whole country-side has met to hunt and kill—at first he bodes no ill, but when some daring youth has struck him with a spear, he crouches open-mouthed, his jaws foam, he roars with fury, he lashes his tail from side to side about his ribs and loins, and glares as he springs straight before him, to find out whether he is to slay, or be slain among the foremost of his foes—even with such fury did Achilles burn to spring upon Æneas.

When they were now close up with one another Achilles was first to speak. "Æneas," said he, "why do you stand thus out before the host to fight me? Is it that you hope to reign over the Trojans in the seat of Priam? Nay, though you kill me Priam will not hand his kingdom over to you. He is a man of sound judgement, and he has sons of his own. Or have the Trojans been allotting you a demesne of passing richness, fair with orchard lawns and corn lands, if you should slay me? This you shall hardly do. I have discomfited you once already. Have you forgotten how when you were alone I chased you from your herds helter-skelter down the slopes of Ida? You did not turn round to look behind you;

you took refuge in Lyrnessus, but I attacked the city, and with the help of Minerva and father Jove I sacked it and carried its women into captivity, though Jove and the other gods rescued you. You think they will protect you now, but they will not do so; therefore I say go back into the host, and do not face me, or you will rue it. Even a fool may be wise after the event."

Then Æneas answered, "Son of Peleus, think not that your words can scare me as though I were a child. I too, if I will, can brag and talk unseemly. We know one another's race and parentage as matters of common fame, though neither have you ever seen my parents nor I yours. Men say that you are son to noble Peleus, and that your mother is Thetis, fair-haired daughter of the sea. I have noble Anchises for my father, and Venus for my mother; the parents of one of other of us shall this day mourn a son, for it will be more than silly talk that shall part us when the fight is over. Learn, then, my lineage if you will—it is known to many.

"In the beginning Dardanus was the son of Jove, and founded Dardania, for Ilius was not yet stablished on the plain for men to dwell in, and her people still abode on the spurs of many-fountained Ida. Dardanus had a son, king Erichthonius, who was wealthiest of all men living; he had three thousand mares that fed by the water-meadows, they and their foals with them. Boreas was enamoured of them as

they were feeding, and covered them in the semblance of a dark-maned stallion. Twelve filly foals
did they conceive and bear him, and these, as they
sped over the rich plain, would go bounding on
over the ripe ears of corn and not break them; or
again when they would disport themselves on the
broad back of Ocean they could gallop on the crest
of a breaker. Erichthonius begat Tros, king of the
Trojans, and Tros had three noble sons, Ilus, Assaracus, and Ganymede who was comeliest of mortal
men; wherefore the gods carried him off to be Jove's
cupbearer, for his beauty's sake, that he might dwell
among the immortals. Ilus begat Laomedon, and
Laomedon begat Tithonus, Priam, Lampus, Clytius,
and Hiketaon of the stock of Mars. But Assaracus
was father to Capys, and Capys to Anchises, who
was my father, while Hector is son to Priam.

"Such do I declare my blood and lineage, but as
for valour, Jove gives it or takes it as he will, for he
is lord of all. And now let there be no more of this
prating in mid-battle as though we were children.
We could fling taunts without end at one another;
a hundred-oared galley would not hold them. The
tongue can run all whithers and talk all wise; it can
go here and there, and as a man says, so shall he be
gainsaid. What is the use of our bandying hard
words, like women who when they fall foul of one
another go out and wrangle in the streets, one half

true and the other lies, as rage inspires them? No words of yours shall turn me now that I am fain to fight—therefore let us make trial of one another with our spears."

As he spoke he drove his spear at the great and terrible shield of Achilles, which rang out as the point struck it. The son of Peleus held the shield before him with his strong hand, and he was afraid, for he deemed that Æneas's spear would go through it quite easily, not reflecting that the god's glorious gifts were little likely to yield before the blows of mortal men; and indeed Æneas's spear did not pierce the shield, for the layer of gold, gift of the god, stayed the point. It went through two layers, but the god had made the shield in five, two of bronze, the two innermost ones of tin, and one of gold; it was in this that the spear was stayed.

Achilles in his turn threw, and struck the round shield of Æneas at the very edge, where the bronze was thinnest; the spear of Pelian ash went clean through, and the shield rang under the blow; Æneas was afraid, and crouched backwards, holding the shield away from him; the spear, however, flew over his back, and stuck quivering in the ground, after having gone through both circles of the sheltering shield. Æneas though he had avoided the spear, stood still, blinded with fear and grief because the weapon had gone so near him; then Achilles sprang furiously upon him, with a cry as of death and with his keen blade drawn, and Æneas seized a great stone, so huge that two men, as men now are, would be unable to lift it, but Æneas wielded it quite easily.

Æneas would then have struck Achilles as he was springing towards him, either on the helmet, or on the shield that covered him, and Achilles would have closed with him and dispatched him with his sword, had not Neptune lord of the earthquake been quick to mark, and said forthwith to the immortals, "Alas, I am sorry for great Æneas, who will now go down to the house of Hades, vanquished by the son of Peleus. Fool that he was to give ear to the counsel of Apollo. Apollo will never save him from destruction. Why should this man suffer when he is guiltless, to no purpose, and in another's quarrel? Has he not at all times offered acceptable sacrifice to the gods that dwell in heaven? Let us then snatch him from death's jaws, lest the son of Saturn be angry should Achilles slay him. It is fated, moreover, that he should escape, and that the race of Dardanus, whom Jove loved above all the sons born to him of mortal women, shall not perish utterly without seed or sign. For now indeed has Jove hated the blood of Priam, while Æneas shall reign over the Trojans, he and his children's children that shall be born hereafter."

Then answered Juno, "Earth-shaker, look to this matter yourself, and consider concerning Æneas, whether you will save him, or suffer him, brave though he be, to fall by the hand of Achilles son of Peleus. For of a truth we two, I and Pallas Minerva, have sworn full many a time before all the immortals, that never would we shield Trojans from destruction, not even when all Troy is burning in the flames that the Achæans shall kindle."

When earth-encircling Neptune heard this he went into the battle amid the clash of spears, and came to the place where Achilles and Æneas were. Forthwith he shed a darkness before the eyes of the son of Peleus, drew the bronze-headed ashen spear from the shield of Æneas, and laid it at the feet of Achilles. Then he lifted Æneas on high from off the earth and hurried him away. Over the heads of many a band of warriors both horse and foot did he soar as the god's hand sped him, till he came to the very fringe of the battle where the Cauconians were arming themselves for fight. Neptune, shaker of the earth, then came near to him and said, "Æneas, what god has egged you on to this folly in fighting the son of Peleus, who is both a mightier man of valour and more beloved of heaven than you are? Give way before him whensoever you meet him, lest you go down to the house of Hades even though fate would have it otherwise. When Achilles is dead you may then fight among the foremost undaunted, for none other of the Achæans shall slay you."

The god left him when he had given him these instructions, and at once removed the darkness from
before the eyes of Achilles, who opened them wide
indeed and said in great anger, "Alas! what marvel
am I now beholding? Here is my spear upon the
ground, but I see not him whom I meant to kill
when I hurled it. Of a truth Æneas also must be
under heaven's protection, although I had thought
his boasting was idle. Let him go hang; he will be in
no mood to fight me further, seeing how narrowly
he has missed being killed. I will now give my orders
to the Danaans and attack some other of the Trojans."

He sprang forward along the line and cheered his
men on as he did so. "Let not the Trojans," he cried,
"keep you at arm's length, Achæans, but go for them
and fight them man for man. However valiant I may
be, I cannot give chase to so many and fight all of
them. Even Mars, who is an immortal, or Minerva,
would shrink from flinging himself into the jaws of
such a fight and laying about him; nevertheless, so
far as in me lies I will show no slackness of hand or
foot nor want of endurance, not even for a moment;
I will utterly break their ranks, and woe to the Trojan who shall venture within reach of my spear."

Thus did he exhort them. Meanwhile Hector
called upon the Trojans and declared that he would
fight Achilles. "Be not afraid, proud Trojans," said he,
"to face the son of Peleus; I could fight gods myself

if the battle were one of words only, but they would be more than a match for me, if we had to use our spears. Even so the deed of Achilles will fall somewhat short of his word; he will do in part, and the other part he will clip short. I will go up against him though his hands be as fire—though his hands be fire and his strength iron."

Thus urged the Trojans lifted up their spears against the Achæans, and raised the cry of battle as they flung themselves into the midst of their ranks. But Phœbus Apollo came up to Hector and said, "Hector, on no account must you challenge Achilles to single combat; keep a lookout for him while you are under cover of the others and away from the thick of the fight, otherwise he will either hit you with a spear or cut you down at close quarters."

Thus he spoke, and Hector drew back within the crowd, for he was afraid when he heard what the god had said to him. Achilles then sprang upon the Trojans with a terrible cry, clothed in valour as with a garment. First he killed Iphition son of Otrynteus, a leader of much people whom a naiad nymph had borne to Otrynteus waster of cities, in the land of Hydè under the snowy heights of Mt. Tmolus. Achilles struck him full on the head as he was coming on towards him, and split it clean in two; whereon he fell heavily to the ground and Achilles vaunted over him saying, "You lie now, son of

Otrynteus, mighty hero; your death is here, but your lineage is on the Gygæan lake where your father's estate lies, by Hyllus, rich in fish, and the eddying waters of Hermus."

Thus did he vaunt, but darkness closed the eyes of the other. The chariots of the Achæans cut him up as their wheels passed over him in the front of the battle, and after him Achilles killed Demoleon, a valiant man of war and son to Antenor. He struck him on the temple through his bronze-cheeked helmet. The helmet did not stay the spear, but it went right on, crushing the bone so that the brain inside was shed in all directions, and his lust of fighting was ended. Then he struck Hippodamas in the midriff as he was springing down from his chariot in front of him, and trying to escape. He breathed his last, bellowing like a bull bellows when young men are dragging him to offer him in sacrifice to the King of Helice, and the heart of the earth-shaker is glad: even so did he bellow as he lay dying. Achilles then went in pursuit of Polydorus son of Priam, whom his father had always forbidden to fight because he was the youngest of his sons, the one he loved best, and the fastest runner. He, in his folly and showing off the fleetness of his feet, was rushing about among the front ranks until he lost his life, for Achilles struck him in the middle of the back as he was darting past him: he struck him just at the golden fastenings of his belt and where the two pieces of the double breastplate overlapped. The point of the spear pierced him through and came out by the navel, whereon he fell groaning on his knees and a cloud of darkness overshadowed him as he sank holding his entrails in his hands.

When Hector saw his brother Polydorus with his entrails in his hands and sinking down upon the ground, a mist came over his eyes, and he could not bear to keep longer at a distance; he therefore poised his spear and darted towards Achilles like a flame of fire. When Achilles saw him he bounded forward and vaunted saying, "This is he that has wounded my heart most deeply and has slain my beloved comrade. Not for long shall we two quail before one another on the highways of war."

He looked fiercely on Hector and said, "Draw near, that you may meet your doom the sooner." Hector feared him not and answered, "Son of Peleus, think not that your words can scare me as though I were a child; I too if I will can brag and talk unseemly; I know that you are a mighty warrior, mightier by far than I, nevertheless the issue lies in the lap of heaven whether I, worse man though I be, may not slay you with my spear, for this too has been found keen ere now."

He hurled his spear as he spoke, but Minerva breathed upon it, and though she breathed but very

lightly she turned it back from going towards
Achilles, so that it returned to Hector and lay at his
feet in front of him. Achilles then sprang furiously
upon him with a loud cry, bent on killing him, but
Apollo caught him up easily as a god can, and hid
him in a thick darkness. Thrice did Achilles spring
towards him spear in hand, and thrice did he waste
his blow upon the air. When he rushed forward
for the fourth time as though he were a god, he
shouted aloud saying, "Hound, this time too you
have escaped death—but of a truth it came exceed-
ingly near you. Phœbus Apollo, to whom it seems
you pray before you go into battle, has again saved
you; but if I too have any friend among the gods I
will surely make an end of you when I come across
you at some other time. Now, however, I will pursue and overtake other Trojans."

On this he struck Dryops with his spear, about
the middle of his neck, and he fell headlong at his
feet. There he let him lie and stayed Demouchus son
of Philetor, a man both brave and of great stature, by
hitting him on the knee with a spear; then he smote
him with his sword and killed him. After this he
sprang on Laogonus and Dardanus, sons of Bias, and
threw them from their chariot, the one with a blow
from a thrown spear, while the other he cut down
in hand-to-hand fight. There was also Tros the son
of Alastor—he came up to Achilles and clasped his

knees in the hope that he would spare him and not kill him but let him go, because they were both of the same age. Fool, he might have known that he should not prevail with him, for the man was in no mood for pity or forbearance but was in grim earnest. Therefore when Tros laid hold of his knees and sought a hearing for his prayers, Achilles drove his sword into his liver, and the liver came rolling out, while his bosom was all covered with the black blood that welled from the wound. Thus did death close his eyes as he lay lifeless.

Achilles then went up to Mulius and struck him on the ear with a spear, and the bronze spear-head came right out at the other ear. He also struck Echeclus son of Agenor on the head with his sword, which became warm with the blood, while death and stern fate closed the eyes of Echeclus. Next in order the bronze point of his spear wounded Deucalion in the fore-arm where the sinews of the elbow are united, whereon he waited Achilles' onset with his arm hanging down and death staring him in the face. Achilles cut his head off with a blow from his sword and flung it helmet and all away from him, and the marrow came oozing out of his backbone as he lay. He then went in pursuit of Rhigmus, noble son of Peires, who had come from fertile Thrace, and struck him through the middle with a spear which fixed itself in his belly, so that he fell headlong from his chariot. He also speared Areïthous squire to Rhigmus in the back as he was turning his horses in flight, and thrust him from his chariot, while the horses were struck with panic.

As a fire raging in some mountain glen after long drought—and the dense forest is in a blaze, while the wind carries great tongues of fire in every direction—even so furiously did Achilles rage, wielding his spear as though he were a god, and giving chase to those whom he would slay, till the dark earth ran with blood. Or as one who yokes broad-browed oxen that they may tread barley in a threshing-floor—and it is soon bruised small under the feet of the lowing cattle—even so did the horses of Achilles trample on the shields and bodies of the slain. The axle underneath and the railing that ran round the car were bespattered with clots of blood thrown up by the horses' hoofs, and from the tyres of the wheels; but the son of Peleus pressed on to win still further glory, and his hands were bedrabbled with gore.

BOOK XXI

Now when they came to the ford of the full-flowing river Xanthus, begotten of immortal Jove, Achilles cut their forces in two: one half he chased over the plain towards the city by the same way that the Achæans had taken when flying panic-stricken on the preceding day with Hector in full triumph; this way did they fly pell-mell, and Juno sent down a thick mist in front of them to stay them. The other half were hemmed in by the deep silver-eddying stream, and fell into it with a great uproar. The waters resounded, and the banks rang again, as they swam hither and thither with loud cries amid the whirling eddies. As locusts flying to a river before the blast of a grass fire—the flame comes on and on till at last it overtakes them and they huddle into the water—even so was the eddying stream of Xanthus filled with the uproar of men and horses, all struggling in confusion before Achilles.

Forthwith the hero left his spear upon the bank, leaning it against a tamarisk bush, and plunged into the river like a god, armed with his sword only. Fell was his purpose as he hewed the Trojans down on every side. Their dying groans rose hideous as the sword smote them, and the river ran red with blood. As when fish fly scared before a huge dolphin, and fill every nook and corner of some fair haven—for he is sure to eat all he can catch—even so did the Trojans cower under the banks of the mighty river, and when Achilles' arms grew weary with killing them, he drew twelve youths alive out of the water, to sacrifice in revenge for Patroclus son of Menœtius. He drew them out like dazed fawns, bound their hands behind them with the girdles of their own shirts, and gave them over to his men to take back to the ships. Then he sprang into the river, thirsting for still further blood.

There he found Lycaon, son of Priam seed of Dardanus, as he was escaping out of the water; he it was whom he had once taken prisoner when he was in his father's vineyard, having set upon him by night, as he was cutting young shoots from a wild fig-tree to make the wicker sides of a chariot. Achilles then caught him to his sorrow unawares, and sent him by sea to Lemnos, where the son of Jason bought him. But a guest-friend, Eëtion of Imbros, freed him with a great sum, and sent him to Arisbe, whence he had escaped and returned to his father's house. He had spent eleven days happily with his friends after he had come from Lemnos, but on the twelfth heaven again delivered him into the hands of Achilles, who was to send him to the house of Hades sorely against his will. He was unarmed when Achilles caught sight of him, and had neither helmet nor shield; nor yet had he any spear, for he had thrown all his armour from him on to the bank, and was sweating with his struggles to get out of the river, so that his strength was now failing him.

Then Achilles said to himself in his surprise, "What marvel do I see here? If this man can come back alive after having been sold over into Lemnos, I shall have the Trojans also whom I have slain rising from the world below. Could not even the waters of the grey sea imprison him, as they do many another whether he will or no? This time let him taste my spear, that I may know for certain whether mother earth who can keep even a strong man down, will be able to hold him, or whether thence too he will return."

Thus did he pause and ponder. But Lycaon came up to him dazed and trying hard to embrace his knees, for he would fain live, not die. Achilles thrust at him with his spear, meaning to kill him, but Lycaon ran crouching up to him and caught his knees, whereby the spear passed over his back, and stuck in the ground, hungering though it was for blood. With one hand he caught Achilles' knees as he besought him, and with the other he clutched the spear and would not let it go. Then he said, "Achilles, have mercy upon me and spare me, for I am your suppliant. It was in your tents that I first broke bread on the day when you took me prisoner in the vineyard; after which you sold me away to Lemnos far from my father and my friends, and I brought you the price of a hundred oxen. I have paid three times as much to gain my freedom; it is but twelve days that I have come to Ilius after much suffering, and now cruel fate has again thrown me into your hands. Surely father Jove must hate me, that he has given me over to you a second time. Short of life indeed

did my mother Laothöe bear me, daughter of aged
Altes—of Altes who reigns over the warlike Lelegæ
and holds steep Pedasus on the river Satniöeis. Priam
married his daughter along with many other women
and two sons were born of her, both of whom you
will have slain. Your spear slew noble Polydorus as he
was fighting in the front ranks, and now evil will
here befall me, for I fear that I shall not escape you
since heaven has delivered me over to you. Furthermore I say, and lay my saying to your heart, spare me,
for I am not of the same womb as Hector who slew
your brave and noble comrade."

With such words did the princely son of Priam
beseech Achilles; but Achilles answered him sternly.
"Idiot," said he, "talk not to me of ransom. Until Patroclus fell I preferred to give the Trojans quarter,
and sold beyond the sea many of those whom I had
taken alive; but now not a man shall live of those
whom heaven delivers into my hands before the city
of Ilius—and of all Trojans it shall fare hardest with
the sons of Priam. Therefore, my friend, you too
shall die. Why should you whine in this way? Patroclus fell, and he was a better man than you are. I
too—see you not how I am great and goodly? I am
son to a noble father, and have a goddess for my
mother, but the hands of doom and death over-
shadow me all as surely. The day will come, either at
dawn or dark, or at the noontide, when one shall

take my life also in battle, either with his spear, or with an arrow sped from his bow."

Thus did he speak, and Lycaon's heart sank within him. He loosed his hold of the spear, and held out both hands before him; but Achilles drew his keen blade, and struck him by the collar-bone on his neck; he plunged his two-edged sword into him to the very hilt, whereon he lay at full length on the ground, with the dark blood welling from him till the earth was soaked. Then Achilles caught him by the foot and flung him into the river to go down stream, vaunting over him the while, and saying, "Lie there among the fishes, who will lick the blood from your wound and gloat over it; your mother shall not lay you on any bier to mourn you, but the eddies of Scamander shall bear you into the broad bosom of the sea. There shall the fishes feed on the fat of Lycaon as they dart under the dark ripple of the waters—so perish all of you till we reach the citadel of strong Ilius—you in flight, and I following after to destroy you. The river with its broad silver stream shall serve you in no stead, for all the bulls you offered him and all the horses that you flung living into his waters. None the less miserably shall you perish till there is not a man of you but has paid in full for the death of Patroclus and the havoc you wrought among the Achæans whom you have slain while I held aloof from battle."

So spoke Achilles, but the river grew more and more angry, and pondered within himself how he should stay the hand of Achilles and save the Trojans from disaster.

Meanwhile the son of Peleus, spear in hand, sprang upon Asteropæus son of Pelegon to kill him. He was son to the broad river Axius and Peribœa eldest daughter of Acessamenus; for the river had lain with her. Asteropæus stood up out of the water to face him with a spear in either hand, and Xanthus filled him with courage, being angry for the death of the youths whom Achilles was slaying ruthlessly within his waters. When they were close up with one another Achilles was first to speak. "Who and whence are you," said he, "who dare to face me? Woe to the parents whose son stands up against me." And the son of Pelegon answered, "Great son of Peleus, why should you ask my lineage. I am from the fertile land of far Pæonia, captain of the Pæonians, and it is now eleven days that I am at Ilius. I am of the blood of the river Axius—of Axius that is the fairest of all rivers that run. He begot the famed warrior Pelegon, whose son men call me. Let us now fight, Achilles."

Thus did he defy him, and Achilles raised his spear of Pelian ash. Asteropæus failed with both his spears, for he could use both hands alike; with the one spear he struck Achilles' shield, but did not pierce it, for the layer of gold, gift of the god, stayed the point; with the other spear he grazed the elbow of Achilles' right arm drawing dark blood, but the spear itself went by him and fixed itself in the ground, foiled of its bloody banquet. Then Achilles, fain to kill him, hurled his spear at Asteropæus, but failed to hit him and struck the steep back of the river, driving the spear half its length into the earth. The son of Peleus then drew his sword and sprang furiously upon him. Asteropæus vainly tried to draw Achilles' spear out of the bank by main force; thrice did he tug at it, trying with all his might to draw it out, and thrice he had to leave off trying; the fourth time he tried to bend and break it, but ere he could do so Achilles smote him with his sword and killed him. He struck him in the belly near the navel, so that all his bowels came gushing out on to the ground, and the darkness of death came over him as he lay gasping. Then Achilles set his foot on his chest and spoiled him of his armour, vaunting over him and saying, "Lie there—begotten of a river though you be, it is hard for you to strive with the offspring of Saturn's son. You declare yourself sprung from the blood of a broad river, but I am of the seed of mighty Jove. My father is Peleus, son of Æacus ruler over the many Myrmidons, and Æacus was the son of Jove. Therefore as Jove is mightier than any river that flows into the sea, so are his children stronger than those of any river whatsoever. Moreover you have a great river hard by if he can be of any use to you, but there is no fighting against Jove the son of Saturn, with whom not even King Achelous can compare, nor the mighty stream of deep-flowing Oceanus, from whom all rivers and seas with all springs and deep wells proceed; even Oceanus fears the lightnings of great Jove, and his thunder that comes crashing out of heaven."

With this he drew his bronze spear out of the bank, and now that he had killed Asteropæus, he let him lie where he was on the sand, with the dark water flowing over him and the eels and fishes busy nibbling and gnawing the fat that was about his kidneys. Then he went in chase of the Pæonians, who were flying along the bank of the river in panic when they saw their leader slain by the hands of the son of Peleus. Therein he slew Thersilochus, Mydon, Astypylus, Mnesus, Thrasius, Œneus, and Ophelestes, and he would have slain yet others, had not the river in anger taken human form, and spoken to him from out the deep waters saying, "Achilles, if you excel all in strength, so do you also in wickedness, for the gods are ever with you to protect you: if, then, the son of Saturn has vouchsafed it to you to destroy all the Trojans, at any rate drive them out of my stream, and do your grim work on land. My fair waters are now filled with corpses, nor can I find any channel by which I may pour myself into the sea for I am choked with dead, and yet you go on mercilessly slaying. I am in despair, therefore, O captain of your host, trouble me no further."

Achilles answered, "So be it, Scamander, Jove-descended; but I will never cease dealing out death among the Trojans, till I have pent them up in their city, and made trial of Hector face to face, that I may learn whether he is to vanquish me, or I him."

As he spoke he set upon the Trojans with a fury like that of the gods. But the river said to Apollo, "Surely, son of Jove, lord of the silver bow, you are not obeying the commands of Jove who charged you straitly that you should stand by the Trojans and defend them, till twilight fades, and darkness is over all the earth."

Meanwhile Achilles sprang from the bank into mid-stream, whereon the river raised a high wave and attacked him. He swelled his stream into a torrent, and swept away the many dead whom Achilles had slain and left within his waters. These he cast out on to the land, bellowing like a bull the while, but the living he saved alive, hiding them in his mighty eddies. The great and terrible wave gathered about Achilles, falling upon him and beating on his shield, so that he could not keep his feet; he caught hold of a great elm-tree, but it came up by the roots, and tore away the bank, damming the stream with its thick branches and bridging it all across; whereby

Achilles struggled out of the stream, and fled full
speed over the plain, for he was afraid.

But the mighty god ceased not in his pursuit, and
sprang upon him with a dark-crested wave, to stay
his hands and save the Trojans from destruction. The
son of Peleus darted away a spear's throw from him;
swift as the swoop of a black hunter-eagle which is
the strongest and fleetest of all birds, even so did he
spring forward, and the armour rang loudly about
his breast. He fled on in front, but the river with a
loud roar came tearing after. As one who would
water his garden leads a stream from some fountain
over his plants, and all his ground—spade in hand he
clears away the dams to free the channels, and the little stones run rolling round and round with the
water as it goes merrily down the bank faster than
the man can follow—even so did the river keep
catching up with Achilles albeit he was a fleet runner, for the gods are stronger than men. As often as
he would strive to stand his ground, and see whether
or not all the gods in heaven were in league against
him, so often would the mighty wave come beating
down upon his shoulders, and he would have to
keep flying on and on in great dismay; for the angry
flood was tiring him out as it flowed past him, and
ate the ground from under his feet.

Then the son of Peleus lifted up his voice to heaven
saying, "Father Jove, is there none of the gods who

will take pity upon me, and save me from the river? I do not care what may happen to me afterwards. I blame none of the other dwellers on Olympus so severely as I do my dear mother, who has beguiled and tricked me. She told me I was to fall under the walls of Troy by the flying arrows of Apollo; would that Hector, the best man among the Trojans, might there slay me; then should I fall a hero by the hand of a hero; whereas now it seems that I shall come to a most pitiable end, trapped in this river as though I were some swineherd's boy, who gets carried down a torrent while trying to cross it during a storm."

As soon as he had spoken thus, Neptune and Minerva came up to him in the likeness of two men, and took him by the hand to reassure him. Neptune spoke first. "Son of Peleus," said he, "be not so exceeding fearful; we are two gods, come with Jove's sanction to assist you, I, and Pallas Minerva. It is not your fate to perish in this river; he will abate presently as you will see; moreover we strongly advise you, if you will be guided by us, not to stay your hand from fighting till you have pent the Trojan host within the famed walls of Ilius—as many of them as may escape. Then kill Hector and go back to the ships, for we will vouchsafe you a triumph over him."

When they had so said they went back to the other immortals, but Achilles strove onward over the plain, encouraged by the charge the gods had laid upon him. All was now covered with the flood of waters, and much goodly armour of the youths that had been slain was drifting about, as also many corpses, but he forced his way against the stream, speeding right onwards, nor could the broad waters stay him, for Minerva had endowed him with great strength. Nevertheless Scamander did not slacken in his pursuit, but was still more furious with the son of Peleus. He lifted his waters into a high crest and cried aloud to Simois saying, "Dear brother, let the two of us unite to stay this man, or he will sack the mighty city of King Priam, and the Trojans will not hold out against him. Help me at once; fill your streams with water from their sources, rouse all your torrents to a fury; raise your wave on high, and let snags and stones come thundering down you that we may make an end of this savage creature who is now lording it as though he were a god. Nothing shall serve him longer, not strength nor comeliness, nor his fine armour, which forsooth shall soon be lying low in the deep waters covered over with mud. I will wrap him in sand, and pour tons of shingle round him, so that the Achæans shall not know how to gather his bones for the silt in which I shall have hidden him, and when they celebrate his funeral they need build no barrow."

On this he upraised his tumultuous flood high against Achilles, seething as it was with foam and blood and the bodies of the dead. The dark waters of the river stood upright and would have over-whelmed the son of Peleus, but Juno, trembling lest Achilles should be swept away in the mighty torrent, lifted her voice on high and called out to Vulcan her son. "Crook-foot," she cried, "my child, be up and doing, for I deem it is with you than Xanthus is fain to fight; help us at once, kindle a fierce fire; I will then bring up the west and the white south wind in a mighty hurricane from the sea, that shall bear the flames against the heads and armour of the Trojans and consume them, while you go along the banks of Xanthus burning his trees and wrapping him round with fire. Let him not turn you back neither by fair words nor foul, and slacken not till I shout and tell you. Then you may stay your flames."

On this Vulcan kindled a fierce fire, which broke out first upon the plain and burned the many dead whom Achilles had killed and whose bodies were lying about in great numbers; by this means the plain was dried and the flood stayed. As the north wind, blowing on an orchard that has been sodden with autumn rain, soon dries it, and the heart of the owner is glad—even so the whole plain was dried and the dead bodies were consumed. Then he turned tongues of fire on to the river. He burned the elms the willows and the tamarisks, the lotus also, with the rushes and marshy herbage that grew abundantly by the banks of the river. The eels and fishes that go darting about everywhere in the water, these, too, were sorely harassed by the flames that cunning Vulcan had kindled, and the river himself was scalded, so that he spoke saying, "Vulcan, there is no god can hold his own against you. I cannot fight you when you flare out your flames in this way; strive with me no longer. Let Achilles drive the Trojans out of their city immediately. What have I to do with quarreling and helping people?"

He was boiling as he spoke, and all his waters were seething. As a cauldron upon a large fire boils when it is melting the lard of some fatted hog, and the lard keeps bubbling up all over when the dry faggots blaze under it—even so were the goodly waters of Xanthus heated with the fire till they were boiling. He could flow no longer but stayed his stream, so afflicted was he by the blasts of fire which cunning Vulcan had raised. Then he prayed to Juno and besought her saying, "Juno, why should your son vex my stream with such especial fury? I am not so much to blame as all the others are who have been helping the Trojans. I will leave off, since you so desire it, and let your son leave off also. Furthermore I swear that never again will I do anything to save the Trojans from destruction, not even when all Troy is burning in the flames which the Achæans will kindle."

As soon as Juno heard this she said to her son Vulcan, "Son Vulcan, hold now your flames; we ought not to use such violence against a god for the sake of mortals."

When she had thus spoken Vulcan quenched his flames, and the river went back once more into his own fair bed.

Xanthus was now beaten, so these two left off fighting, for Juno stayed them though she was still angry; but a furious quarrel broke out among the other gods, for they were of divided counsels. They fell on one another with a mighty uproar—earth groaned, and the spacious firmament rang out as with a blare of trumpets. Jove heard as he was sitting on Olympus, and laughed for joy when he saw the gods coming to blows among themselves. They were not long about beginning, and Mars piercer of shields opened the battle. Sword in hand he sprang at once upon Minerva and reviled her. "Why, vixen," said he, "have you again set the gods by the ears in the pride and haughtiness of your heart? Have you forgotten how you set Diomed son of Tydeus on to wound me, and yourself took visible spear and drove it into me to the hurt of my fair body? You shall now suffer for what you then did to me."

As he spoke he struck her on the terrible tasselled ægis—so terrible that not even can Jove's lightning pierce it. Here did murderous Mars strike her with his great spear. She drew back and with her strong hand seized a stone that was lying on the plain—great and rugged and black—which men of old had set for the boundary of a field. With this she struck Mars on the neck, and brought him down. Nine roods did he cover in his fall, and his hair was all soiled in the dust, while his armour rang rattling round him. But Minerva laughed and vaunted over him saying, "Idiot, have you not learned how far stronger I am than you, but you must still match yourself against me? Thus do your mother's curses now roost upon you, for she is angry and would do you mischief because you have deserted the Achæans and are helping the Trojans."

She then turned her two piercing eyes elsewhere, whereon Jove's daughter Venus took Mars by the hand and led him away, groaning all the time, for it was only with great difficulty that he had come to himself again. When Queen Juno saw her, she said to Minerva, "Look, daughter of ægis-bearing Jove, unweariable, that vixen Venus is again taking Mars through the crowd out of the battle; go after her at once."

Thus she spoke. Minerva sped after Venus with a will, and made at her, striking her on the bosom with her strong hand so that she fell fainting to the ground, and there they both lay stretched at full length. Then Minerva vaunted over her saying,

"May all who help the Trojans against the Argives prove just as redoubtable and stalwart as Venus did when she came across me while she was helping Mars. Had this been so, we should long since have ended the war by sacking the strong city of Ilius."

Juno smiled as she listened. Meanwhile King Neptune turned to Apollo saying, "Phœbus, why should we keep each other at arm's length? It is not well, now that the others have begun fighting; it will be disgraceful to us if we return to Jove's bronze-floored mansion on Olympus without having fought each other; therefore come on, you are the younger of the two, and I ought not to attack you, for I am older and have had more experience. Idiot, you have no sense, and forget how we two alone of all the gods fared hardly round about Ilius when we came from Jove's house and worked for Laomedon a whole year at a stated wage and he gave us his orders. I built the Trojans the wall about their city, so wide and fair that it might be impregnable, while you, Phœbus, herded cattle for him in the dales of many-valleyed Ida. When, however, the glad hours brought round the time of payment, mighty Laomedon robbed us of all our hire and sent us off with nothing but abuse. He threatened to bind us hand and foot and sell us over into some distant island. He tried, moreover, to cut off the ears of both of us, so we went away in a rage, furious about the payment he had promised us, and yet withheld; in spite of all this, you are now showing favour to his people, and will not join us in compassing the utter ruin of the proud Trojans with their wives and children."

And King Apollo answered, "Lord of the earthquake, you would have no respect for me if I were to fight you about a pack of miserable mortals, who come out like leaves in summer and eat the fruit of the field, and presently fall lifeless to the ground. Let us stay this fighting at once and let them settle it among themselves."

He turned away as he spoke, for he would lay no hand on the brother of his own father. But his sister the huntress Diana, patroness of wild beasts, was very angry with him and said, "So you would fly, Far-Darter, and hand victory over to Neptune with a cheap vaunt to boot. Baby, why keep your bow thus idle? Never let me again hear you bragging in my father's house, as you often have done in the presence of the immortals, that you would stand up and fight with Neptune."

Apollo made her no answer, but Jove's august queen was angry and upbraided her bitterly. "Bold vixen," she cried, "how dare you cross me thus? For all your bow you will find it hard to hold your own against me. Jove made you as a lion among women, and lets you kill them whenever you choose. You will find it better to chase wild beasts and deer upon the mountains than to fight those who are stronger than you are. If you would try war, do so, and find out by pitting yourself against me, how far stronger I am than you are."

She caught both Diana's wrists with her left hand as she spoke, and with her right she took the bow from her shoulders, and laughed as she beat her with it about the ears while Diana wriggled and writhed under her blows. Her swift arrows were shed upon the ground, and she fled weeping from under Juno's hand as a dove that flies before a falcon to the cleft of some hollow rock, when it is her good fortune to escape. Even so did she fly weeping away, leaving her bow and arrows behind her.

Then the slayer of Argus, guide and guardian, said to Leto, "Leto, I shall not fight you; it is ill to come to blows with any of Jove's wives. Therefore boast as you will among the immortals that you worsted me in fair fight."

Leto then gathered up Diana's bow and arrows that had fallen about amid the whirling dust, and when she had got them she made all haste after her daughter. Diana had now reached Jove's bronze-floored mansion on Olympus, and sat herself down with many tears on the knees of her father, while her ambrosial raiment was quivering all about her. The son of Saturn drew her towards him, and laughing pleasantly the while began to question her saying,

"Which of the heavenly beings, my dear child, has been treating you in this cruel manner, as though you had been misconducting yourself in the face of everybody?" and the fair-crowned goddess of the chase answered, "It was your wife Juno, father, who has been beating me; it is always her doing when there is any quarrelling among the immortals."

Thus did they converse, and meanwhile Phœbus Apollo entered the strong city of Ilius, for he was uneasy lest the wall should not hold out and the Danaans should take the city then and there, before its hour had come; but the rest of the ever-living gods went back, some angry and some triumphant to Olympus, where they took their seats beside Jove lord of the storm-cloud, while Achilles still kept on dealing out death alike on the Trojans and on their horses. As when the smoke from some burning city ascends to heaven when the anger of the gods has kindled it—there is then toil for all, and sorrow for not a few—even so did Achilles bring toil and sorrow on the Trojans.

Old King Priam stood on a high tower of the wall looking down on huge Achilles as the Trojans fled panic-stricken before him, and there was none to help them. Presently he came down from off the tower and with many a groan went along the wall to give orders to the brave warders of the gate. "Keep the gates," said he, "wide open till the people come flying into the city, for Achilles is hard by and is driving them in rout before him. I see we are in great peril. As soon as our people are inside and in safety, close the strong gates for I fear lest that terrible man should come bounding inside along with the others."

As he spoke they drew back the bolts and opened the gates, and when these were opened there was a haven of refuge for the Trojans. Apollo then came full speed out of the city to meet them and protect them. Right for the city and the high wall, parched with thirst and grimy with dust, still they fled on, with Achilles wielding his spear furiously behind them. For he was as one possessed, and was thirsting after glory.

Then had the sons of the Achæans taken the lofty gates of Troy if Apollo had not spurred on Agenor, valiant and noble son to Antenor. He put courage into his heart, and stood by his side to guard him, leaning against a beech tree and shrouded in thick darkness. When Agenor saw Achilles he stood still and his heart was clouded with care. "Alas," said he to himself in his dismay, "if I fly before mighty Achilles, and go where all the others are being driven in rout, he will none the less catch me and kill me for a coward. How would it be were I to let Achilles drive the others before him, and then fly from the wall to the plain that is behind Ilius till I reach the spurs of Ida and can hide in the underwood that is thereon? I

could then wash the sweat from off me in the river
and in the evening return to Ilius. But why commune
with myself in this way? Like enough he would see
me as I am hurrying from the city over the plain,
and would speed after me till he had caught me—I
should stand no chance again him, for he is mightiest
of all mankind. What, then, if I go out and meet him
in front of the city? His flesh too, I take it, can be
pierced by pointed bronze. Life is the same in one
and all, and men say that he is but mortal despite the
triumph that Jove son of Saturn vouchsafes him."

So saying he stood on his guard and awaited
Achilles, for he was now fain to fight him. As a leop-
ardess that bounds from out a thick covert to attack
a hunter—she knows no fear and is not dismayed by
the baying of the hounds; even though the man be
too quick for her and wound her either with thrust
or spear, still, though the spear has pierced her she
will not give in till she has either caught him in her
grip or been killed outright—even so did noble
Agenor son of Antenor refuse to fly till he had made
trial of Achilles, and took aim at him with his spear,
holding his round shield before him and crying
with a loud voice. "Of a truth," said he, "noble
Achilles, you deem that you shall this day sack the
city of the proud Trojans. Fool, there will be trouble
enough yet before it, for there is many a brave man
of us still inside who will stand in front of our dear

parents with our wives and children, to defend Ilius.
Here therefore, huge and mighty warrior though
you be, here shall you die."

As he spoke his strong hand hurled his javelin from
him, and the spear struck Achilles on the leg beneath
the knee; the greave of newly wrought tin rang
loudly, but the spear recoiled from the body of him
whom it had struck, and did not pierce it, for the
god's gift stayed it. Achilles in his turn attacked noble
Agenor, but Apollo would not vouchsafe him glory,
for he snatched Agenor away and hid him in a thick
mist, sending him out of the battle unmolested. Then
he craftily drew the son of Peleus away from going
after the host, for he put on the semblance of Agenor
and stood in front of Achilles, who ran towards him
to give him chase and pursued him over the corn
lands of the plain, turning him towards the deep waters of the river Scamander. Apollo ran but a little
way before him and beguiled Achilles by making
him think all the time that he was on the point of
overtaking him. Meanwhile the rabble of routed
Trojans was thankful to crowd within the city till
their numbers thronged it; no longer did they dare
wait for one another outside the city walls, to learn
who had escaped and who were fallen in fight, but
all whose feet and knees could still carry them
poured pell-mell into the town.

Odysseus

[**HOMER**]

And Odysseus answered, "King Alcinous, it is a good thing to hear a bard with such a divine voice as this man has. There is nothing better or more delightful than when a whole people make merry together, with the guests sitting orderly to listen, while the table is loaded with bread and meats, and the cup-bearer draws wine and fills his cup for every man. This is indeed as fair a sight as a man can see. Now, however, since you are inclined to ask the story of my sorrows, and rekindle my own sad memories in respect of them, I do not know how to begin, nor yet how to continue and conclude my tale, for the hand of heaven has been laid heavily upon me.

"Firstly, then, I will tell you my name that you too may know it, and one day, if I outlive this time of sorrow, may become my guests though I live so far away from all of you. I am Odysseus son of Laertes, renowned among mankind for all manner of subtlety, so that my fame ascends to heaven. I live in Ithaca, where there is a high mountain called Neritum, covered with forests; and not far from it there is a group of islands very near to one another—Dulichium, Same, and the wooded island of Zacynthus. It lies squat on the horizon, all highest up in the sea towards the sunset, while the others lie away from it towards dawn. It is a rugged island, but it breeds brave men, and my eyes know none that they better love to look upon. The goddess Calypso kept me with her in her cave, and wanted me to marry her, as did also the cunning Aeaean goddess Circe; but they could neither of them persuade me, for there is nothing dearer to a man than his own country and his parents, and however splendid a home he may have in a foreign country, if it be far from father or mother, he does not care about it. Now, however, I will tell you of the many hazardous adventures which by Zeus' will I met with on my return from Troy.

"When I had set sail thence the wind took me first to Ismarus, which is the city of the Cicones. There I sacked the town and put the people to the sword. We took the wives and also much booty, which we divided equitably amongst us, so that none might have reason to complain. I then said that we had better make off at once, but my men very foolishly would not obey me, so they stayed there drinking much wine and killing great numbers of sheep and oxen on the seashore. Meanwhile the Ciconos cried out for help to other Ciconos who lived inland. These were more in number, and stronger, and they were more skilled in the art of war, for they could fight, either from chariot or on foot as the occasion served. In the morning, therefore, they came as thick as leaves and bloom in summer, and the hand of heaven was against us, so that we were hard pressed. They set the battle in array near the ships, and the hosts aimed their bronze-shod spears at one another. So long as the day waxed and it was still morning, we held our own against them, though they were more in number than we; but as the sun went down, towards the time when men loose their oxen, the Ciconos got the better of us, and we lost half a dozen men from every ship we had; so we got away with those that were left.

"Thence we sailed onward with sorrow in our hearts, but glad to have escaped death though we had lost our comrades, nor did we leave till we had thrice invoked each one of the poor fellows who had perished by the hands of the Ciconos. Then Zeus raised the north wind against us till it blew a hurricane, so that land and sky were hidden in the thick clouds, and night sprang forth out of the heavens. We let the ships run before the gale, but the force of the wind tore our sails to tatters, so we took them down for fear of shipwreck, and rowed our hardest towards the land. There we lay two days and two nights suffering much alike from toil and distress of mind, but on the morning of the third day we again raised our masts, set sail, and took our places, letting the wind and steersmen direct our ship. I should have got home at that time unharmed had not the north wind and the currents been against me as I was doubling Cape Malea, and set me off my course hard by the island of Cythera.

"I was driven thence by foul winds for a space of nine days upon the sea, but on the tenth day we reached the land of the Lotus-eaters, who live on a food that comes from a kind of flower. Here we landed to take in fresh water, and our crews got their midday meal on the shore near the ships. When they had eaten and drunk, I sent two of my company to see what manner of men the people of the place might be, and they had a third man under them. They started at once and went about among the Lotus-eaters, who did them no hurt, but gave them to eat of the lotus, which was so delicious that those who ate of it left off caring about home, and did not even want to go back and say what had happened to them, but were for staying and munching lotus with the Lotus-eaters without thinking further of their return. Nevertheless, though they wept bitterly I forced them back to the ships and made them fast under the benches. Then I told the rest to go on board at once, lest any of them should taste of the lotus and leave off wanting to get home, so they took their places and smote the gray sea with their oars.

"We sailed hence, always in much distress, till we came to the land of the lawless and inhuman Cyclopes. Now the Cyclopes neither plant nor plow, but trust in providence, and live on such wheat, barley, and grapes as grow wild without any kind of tillage, and their wild grapes yield them wine as the sun and the rain may grow them. They have no laws or assemblies of the people, but live in caves on the tops of high mountains; each is lord and master in his family, and they take no account of their neighbors.

"Now off their harbor there lies a wooded and fertile island not quite close to the land of the Cyclopes, but still not far. It is overrun with wild goats, that breed there in great numbers and are never disturbed by foot of man. For sportsmen—who as a rule will suffer so much hardship in forest or among mountain precipices—do not go there, nor yet again is it ever plowed or fed down, but it lies a wilderness untilled and unsown from year to year, and has no living thing upon it but only goats. For the Cyclopes have no ships, nor yet shipwrights who could make ships for them. They cannot therefore go from city to city, or sail over the sea to one another's country as people who have ships can do. If they had had these they would have colonized the island, for it is a very good one, and would yield everything in due season. There are meadows that in some places come right down to the seashore, well watered and full of luscious grass; grapes would do there excellently; there is level land for plowing, and it would always yield heavily at harvest time, for the soil is deep. There is a good harbor where no cables are wanted, nor yet anchors, nor need a ship be moored, but all one has to do is to beach one's vessel and stay there till the wind becomes fair for putting out to sea again. At the head of the harbor there is a spring of clear water coming out of a cave, and there are poplars growing all round it.

"Here we entered, but so dark was the night that some god must have brought us in, for there was nothing whatever to be seen. A thick mist hung all round our ships; the moon was hidden behind a mass of clouds so that no one could have seen the island if he had looked for it, nor were there any breakers to tell us we were close in shore before we found ourselves upon the land itself. When, however, we had beached the ships, we took down the sails, went ashore and camped upon the beach till daybreak.

"When the child of morning, rosy-fingered Dawn, appeared, we admired the island and wandered all over it, while the nymphs, Zeus' daughters, roused the wild goats that we might get some meat for our dinner. On this we fetched our spears and bows and arrows from the ships, and dividing ourselves into three bands began to shoot the goats. Heaven sent us excellent sport; I had twelve ships with me, and each ship got nine goats, while my own ship had ten; thus through the livelong day to the going down of the sun we ate and drank our fill, and we had plenty of wine left, for each one of us had taken many jars full when we sacked the city of the Cicones, and this had not yet run out. While we were feasting we kept turning our eyes towards the land of the Cyclopes, which was hard by, and saw the smoke of their stubble fires. We could almost fancy we heard their voices and the bleating of their sheep and goats, but when the sun went down and it came on dark, we camped down upon the beach, and next morning I called a council.

"'Stay here, my brave fellows,' said I, 'all the rest of you, while I go with my ship and explore these people myself. I want to see if they are uncivilized savages, or a hospitable and humane race.'

"I went on board, bidding my men to do so also and loose the hawsers; so they took their places and smote the gray sea with their oars. When we got to the land, which was not far, there, on the face of a cliff near the sea, we saw a great cave overhung with laurels. It was a station for a great many sheep and goats, and outside there was a large yard, with a high wall round it made of stones built into the ground and of trees both pine and oak. This was the abode of a huge monster who was then away from home shepherding his flocks. He would have nothing to do with other people, but led the life of an outlaw. He was a horrid creature, not like a human being at all, but resembling rather some crag that stands out boldly against the sky on the top of a high mountain.

"I told my men to draw the ship ashore, and stay where they were, all but the twelve best among them, who were to go along with myself. I also took a goatskin of sweet black wine which had been given to me by Maron son of Euanthes, who was priest of Apollo the patron god of Ismarus, and lived within the wooded precincts of the temple. When we were sacking the city we respected him, and spared his life, as also his wife and child; so he made me some presents of great value—seven talents of fine gold, and a bowl of silver, with twelve jars of sweet wine, unblended, and of the most exquisite flavor. Not a man or maid in the house knew about it, but only himself, his wife, and one housekeeper. When he drank it he mixed twenty parts of water to one of wine, and yet the fragrance from the mixing-bowl was so exquisite that it was impossible to refrain from drinking. I filled a large skin with this wine, and took a wallet full of provisions with me, for my mind misgave me that I might have to deal with some savage who would be of great strength, and would respect neither right nor law.

"We soon reached his cave, but he was out shep-herding, so we went inside and took stock of all that we could see. His cheese-racks were loaded with cheeses, and he had more lambs and kids than his pens could hold. They were kept in separate flocks; first there were the hoggets, then the oldest of the younger lambs, and lastly the very young ones, all kept apart from one another. As for his dairy, all the vessels, bowls, and milk pails into which he milked, were swimming with whey. When they saw all this, my men begged me to let them first steal some cheeses, and make off with them to the ship; they would then return, drive down the lambs and kids, put them on board and sail away with them. It would have been indeed better if we had done so, but I would not listen to them, for I wanted to see the owner himself, in the hope that he might give me a present. When, however, we saw him my poor men found him ill to deal with.

"We lit a fire, offered some of the cheeses in sac-rifice, ate others of them, and then sat waiting till the Cyclops should come in with his sheep. When he came, he brought in with him a huge load of dry firewood to light the fire for his supper, and this he flung with such a noise on to the floor of his cave that we hid ourselves for fear at the far end of the cavern. Meanwhile he drove all the ewes inside, as well as the she-goats that he was going to milk, leaving the males, both rams and he-goats, outside in the yards. Then he rolled a huge stone to the mouth of the cave—so huge that two and twenty strong four-wheeled wagons would not be enough to draw it from its place against the doorway. When he had so done he sat down and milked his ewes and goats, all in due course, and then let each of them have her own young. He curdled half the milk and set it aside in wicker strainers, but the other half he poured into bowls that he might drink it for his supper. When he had got through with all his work, he lit the fire, and then caught sight of us, whereon he said:

"'Strangers, who are you? Where do you sail from? Are you traders, or do you sail the sea as rovers, with your hands against every man, and every man's hand against you?'

"We were frightened of our senses by his loud voice and monstrous form, but I managed to say: 'We are Achaeans on our way home from Troy, but by the will of Zeus and stress of weather we have been driven far out of our course. We are the people of Agamemnon son of Atreus, who has won infinite renown throughout the whole world by sacking so great a city and killing so many people. We therefore humbly pray you to show us some hospitality, and otherwise make us such presents as visitors may reasonably expect. May your excellency fear the wrath of heaven, for we are your suppliants, and Zeus takes all respectable travelers under his protection, for he is the avenger of all suppliants and foreigners in distress.'

"To this he gave me but a pitiless answer, 'Stranger,' said he, 'you are a fool, or else you know nothing of this country. Talk to me, indeed, about fearing the gods or shunning their anger? We Cyclopes do not care about Zeus, or any of your blessed gods, for we are ever so much stronger than they. I shall not spare either yourself or your companions out of any regard for Zeus, unless I am in the humor for doing so. And now tell me where you made your ship fast when you came on shore. Was it round the point, or is she lying straight off the land?'

"He said this to draw me out, but I was too cunning to be caught in that way, so I answered with a lie. 'Poseidon,' said I, 'sent my ship on the rocks at the far end of your country, and wrecked it. We were driven onto them from the open sea, but I and those who are with me escaped the jaws of death.'

"The cruel wretch vouchsafed me not one word of answer, but with a sudden clutch he gripped up two of my men at once and dashed them down upon the ground as though they had been puppies. Their brains were shed upon the ground, and the earth was wet with their blood. Then he tore them limb from limb and supped upon them. He gobbled them up like a lion in the wilderness, flesh, bones, marrow, and entrails, without leaving anything un-eaten. As for us, we wept and lifted up our hands to heaven on seeing such a horrid sight, for we did not know what else to do; but when the Cyclops had filled his huge paunch, and had washed down his meal of human flesh with a drink of neat milk, he stretched himself full length upon the ground among his sheep, and went to sleep. I was at first in-clined to seize my sword, draw it, and drive it into his vitals, but I reflected that if I did we should all certainly be lost, for we should never be able to shift the stone which the monster had put in front of the door. So we stayed sobbing and sighing where we were till morning came.

"When the child of morning, rosy-fingered Dawn, appeared, he again lit his fire, milked his goats and ewes, all quite rightly, and then let each have her own young one; as soon as he had got through with all his work, he clutched up two more of my men, and began eating them for his morning's meal. Presently, with the utmost ease, he rolled the stone away from the door and drove out his sheep, but he at once put it back again—as easily as though he were merely clapping the lid on to a quiver full of arrows. As soon as he had done so he shouted and cried, 'Shoo, shoo,' after his sheep to drive them on to the mountain; so I was left to scheme some way of taking my revenge and covering myself with glory.

"In the end I deemed it would be the best plan to do as follows. The Cyclops had a great club which was lying near one of the sheep pens; it was of green olive wood, and he had cut it intending to use it for a staff as soon as it should be dry. It was so huge that we could only compare it to the mast of a twenty-oared merchant vessel of large burden, and able to venture out into open sea. I went up to this club and cut off about six feet of it; I then gave this piece to the men and told them to fine it evenly off at one end, which they proceeded to do, and lastly I brought it to a point myself, charring the end in the fire to make it harder. When I had done this I hid it under the dung, which was lying about all over the cave, and told the men to cast lots which of them should venture along with myself to lift it and bore it into the monster's eye while he was asleep. The lot fell upon the very four whom I should have chosen, and I myself made five. In the evening the wretch came back from shepherding, and drove his flocks into the cave—this time driving them all inside, and not leaving any in the yards; I suppose some fancy must have taken him or a god must have prompted him to do so. As soon as he had put the stone back to its place against the door, he sat down, milked his ewes and his goats all quite rightly, and then let each have her own young one; when he had got through with all this work, he gripped up two more of my men, and made his supper of them. So I went up to him with an ivy-wood bowl of black wine in my hands:

"'Look here, Cyclops,' said I, 'you have been eating a great deal of man's flesh, so take this and drink some wine, that you may see what kind of liquor we had on board my ship. I was bringing it to you as a drink offering, in the hope that you would take compassion upon me and further me on my way home, whereas all you do is to go on ranting and raving most intolerably. You ought to be ashamed of yourself. How can you expect people to come and see you any more if you treat them in this way?'

"He then took the cup and drank. He was so delighted with the taste of the wine that he begged me for another bowl full. 'Be so kind,' he said, 'as to give me some more, and tell me your name at once. I want to make you a present that you will be glad to have. We have wine even in this country, for our soil grows grapes and the sun ripens them, but this drink is like nectar and ambrosia all in one.'

"I then gave him some more; three times did I fill the bowl for him and three times did he drain it without thought or heed. Then, when I saw that the

wine had got into his head, I said to him as plausi-
bly as I could: 'Cyclops, you ask my name and I will
tell it you; give me, therefore, the present you promised me. My name is Noman; this is what my father
and mother and my friends have always called me.'

"But the cruel wretch said, 'Then I will eat all
Noman's comrades before Noman himself, and will
keep Noman for the last. This is the present that I
will make him.'

"As he spoke, he reeled and fell sprawling face
upwards on the ground. His great neck hung heavily backwards and a deep sleep took hold upon him.
Presently he turned sick, and threw up both wine
and the gobbets of human flesh on which he had
been gorging, for he was very drunk. Then I thrust
the beam of wood far into the embers to heat it, and
encouraged my men lest any of them should turn
faint-hearted. When the wood, green though it was,
was about to blaze, I drew it out of the fire glowing
with heat, and my men gathered round me, for
heaven had filled their hearts with courage. We
drove the sharp end of the beam into the monster's
eye, and bearing upon it with all my weight I kept
turning it round and round as though I were boring
a hole in a ship's plank with an auger, which two
men with a wheel and strap can keep on turning as
long as they choose. Even thus did we bore the red-
hot beam into his eye, till the boiling blood bubbled

all over it as we worked it round and round, so that the steam from the burning eyeball scalded his eyelids and eyebrows, and the roots of the eye sputtered in the fire. As a blacksmith plunges an axe or hatchet into cold water to temper it—for it is this that gives strength to the iron—and it makes a great hiss as he does so, even thus did the Cyclops' eye hiss round the beam of olive wood, and his hideous yells made the cave ring again. We ran away in a fright, but he plucked the beam all besmirched with gore from his eye, and hurled it from him in a frenzy of rage and pain, shouting as he did so to the other Cyclopes who lived on the bleak headlands near him. So they gathered from all quarters round his cave when they heard him crying, and asked what was the matter with him.

"'What ails you, Polyphemus,' said they, 'that you make such a noise, breaking the stillness of the night, and preventing us from being able to sleep? Surely no man is carrying off your sheep? Surely no man is trying to kill you either by fraud or by force?'

"But Polyphemus shouted to them from inside the cave, 'Noman is killing me by fraud! Noman is killing me by force!'

"'Then,' said they, 'if no man is attacking you, you must be ill; when Zeus makes people ill, there is no help for it, and you had better pray to your father Poseidon.'

"Then they went away, and I laughed inwardly at the success of my clever stratagem, but the Cyclops, groaning and in an agony of pain, felt about with his hands till he found the stone and took it from the door; then he sat in the doorway and stretched his hands in front of it to catch anyone going out with the sheep, for he thought I might be foolish enough to attempt this.

"As for myself I kept on puzzling to think how I could best save my own life and those of my companions. I schemed and schemed, as one who knows that his life depends upon it, for the danger was very great. In the end I deemed that this plan would be the best. The male sheep were well grown, and carried a heavy black fleece, so I bound them noiselessly in threes together, with some of the withies on which the wicked monster used to sleep. There was to be a man under the middle sheep, and the two on either side were to cover him, so that there were three sheep to each man. As for myself there was a ram finer than any of the others, so I caught hold of him by the back, esconced myself in the thick wool under his belly, and hung on patiently to his fleece, face upwards, keeping a firm hold on it all the time.

"Thus, then, did we wait in great fear of mind till morning came, but when the child of morning, rosy-fingered Dawn, appeared, the male sheep hurried out to feed, while the ewes remained bleating about the pens waiting to be milked, for their udders were full to bursting; but their master, in spite of all his pain, felt the backs of all the sheep as they stood upright, without being sharp enough to find out that the men were underneath their bellies. As the ram was going out, last of all, heavy with its fleece and with the weight of my crafty self, Polyphemus laid hold of it and said:

"'My good ram, what is it that makes you the last to leave my cave this morning? You are not wont to let the ewes go before you, but lead the mob with a run whether to flowery mead or bubbling fountain, and are the first to come home again at night; but now you lag last of all. Is it because you know your master has lost his eye, and are sorry because that wicked Noman and his horrid crew have got him down in his drink and blinded him? But I will have his life yet. If you could understand and talk, you would tell me where the wretch is hiding, and I would dash his brains upon the ground till they flew all over the cave. I should thus have some satisfaction for the harm this no-good Noman has done me.'

"As he spoke he drove the ram outside, but when we were a little way out from the cave and yards, I first got from under the ram's belly, and then freed my comrades; as for the sheep, which were very fat, by constantly heading them in the right direction we managed to drive them down to the ship. The crew

rejoiced greatly at seeing those of us who had escaped death, but wept for the others whom the Cyclops had killed. However, I made signs to them by
nodding and frowning that they were to hush their
crying, and told them to get all the sheep on board
at once and put out to sea. So they went aboard,
took their places, and smote the gray sea with their
oars. Then, when I had got as far out as my voice
would reach, I began to jeer at the Cyclops.

"'Cyclops,' said I, 'you should have taken better
measure of your man before eating up his comrades
in your cave. You wretch, eat up your visitors in your
own house? You might have known that your sin
would find you out, and now Zeus and the other
gods have punished you.'

"He got more and more furious as he heard me,
so he tore the top off from a high mountain, and
flung it just in front of my ship so that it was within
a little of hitting the end of the rudder. The sea
quaked as the rock fell into it, and the wash of the
wave it raised carried us back towards the mainland,
and forced us towards the shore. But I snatched up
a long pole and kept the ship off, making signs to
my men by nodding my head, that they must row
for their lives, whereon they laid out with a will.
When we had got twice as far as we were before, I
was for jeering at the Cyclops again, but the men
begged and prayed of me to hold my tongue.

"'Do not,' they exclaimed, 'be mad enough to provoke this savage creature further. He has thrown one rock at us already which drove us back again to the mainland, and we made sure it had been the death of us. If he had then heard any further sound of voices he would have pounded our heads and our ship's timbers into a jelly with the rugged rocks he would have heaved at us, for he can throw them a long way.'"

"But I would not listen to them, and shouted out to him in my rage, 'Cyclops, if anyone asks you who it was that put your eye out and spoiled your beauty, say it was the valiant warrior Odysseus son of Laertes, who lives in Ithaca.'"

"On this he groaned, and cried out, 'Alas, alas, then the old prophecy about me is coming true. There was a prophet here, at one time, a man both brave and of great stature, Telemus son of Eurymus, who was an excellent seer, and did all the prophesying for the Cyclopes till he grew old. He told me that all this would happen to me some day, and said I should lose my sight by the hand of Odysseus. I have been all along expecting someone of imposing presence and superhuman strength, whereas he turns out to be a little insignificant weakling, who has managed to blind my eye by taking advantage of me in my drink. Come here, then, Odysseus, that I may make you presents to show my hospitality, and urge Poseidon to help you forward on your journey—for Poseidon and I are father and son. He, if he so will, shall heal me, which no one else neither god nor man can do.'

"Then I said, 'I wish I could be as sure of killing you outright and sending you down to the house of Hades, as I am that it will take more than Poseidon to cure that eye of yours.'

"On this he lifted up his hands to the firmament of heaven and prayed, saying: 'Hear me, great Poseidon! If I am indeed your own true-begotten son, grant that Odysseus may never reach his home alive; or if he must get back to his friends at last, let him do so late and in sore plight after losing all his men. Let him reach his home in another man's ship and find trouble in his house.'

"Thus did he pray, and Poseidon heard his prayer. Then he picked up a rock much larger than the first, swung it aloft and hurled it with prodigious force. It fell just short of the ship, but was within a little of hitting the end of the rudder. The sea quaked as the rock fell into it, and the wash of the wave it raised drove us onwards on our way towards the shore of the island.

"When at last we got to the island where we had left the rest of our ships, we found our comrades lamenting us and anxiously awaiting our return. We ran our vessel upon the sands and got out of her on to the seashore. We also landed the Cyclops' sheep, and divided them equitably amongst us so that none might have reason to complain. As for the ram, my companions agreed that I should have it as an extra share; so I sacrificed it on the seashore, and burned its thighbones to Zeus, who is the lord of all. But he heeded not my sacrifice, and only thought how he might destroy both my ships and my comrades.

"Thus through the livelong day to the going down of the sun we feasted our fill on meat and drink, but when the sun went down and it came on dark, we camped upon the beach. When the child of morning, rosy-fingered Dawn, appeared, I bade my men go on board and loose the hawsers. Then they took their places and smote the gray sea with their oars; so we sailed on with sorrow in our hearts, but glad to have escaped death though we had lost our comrades."

Beowulf

[JOHN EARLE]

What ho! we have heard tell of the grandeur of the imperial kings of the spear-bearing Danes in former days, how those ethelings promoted bravery. Often did Scyld of the Sheaf wrest from harrying bands, from many tribes, their convivial seats; the dread of him fell upon warriors, whereas he had at the first been a lonely foundling;—of all that (humiliation) he lived to experience solace; he waxed great under the welkin, he flourished with trophies, till that every one of the neighbouring peoples over the sea were constrained to obey him and pay trewage:—that was a good king!

To him was born a son to come after him, a young (prince) in the palace, whom God sent for the people's comfort. He (God) knew the hard calamity, what they had erst endured when they were without a king for a long while; and in consideration thereof the Lord of Life, the Ruler of Glory accorded to them a time of prosperity.

Beowulf (i.e. Beaw) was renowned, his fame sprang wide; heir of Scyld in the Scedelands. So Ought a young chief to work with his wealth, with gracious largesses, while in his father's nurture; that in his riper age willing comrades may in return stand by him at the coming of war, and that men may do his bidding. Eminence must, in every nation, be attained by deeds (worthy) of praise.

As for Scyld, he departed, at the destined hour, full of exploit, to go into the Master's keeping. They then carried him forth to the shore of the sea, his faithful comrades, as he himself had requested, while he with his words held sway as lord of the Scyldings; dear chief of the land, he had long tenure of power.

There at hythe stood the ship with ringèd prow, glistening fresh, and outward bound; convoy for a prince. Down laid they there the lovèd chief, dispenser of jewels, on the lap of the ship, the illustrious (dead) by the mast. There was store of precious things, ornaments from remote parts, brought together; never heard I of craft comelier fitted with slaughter weapons and campaigning harness, with bills and breast-mail:—in his keeping lay a multitude of treasures, which were to pass with him far away into the watery realm. Not at all with less gifts, less stately opulence, did they outfit him, than those had done who at the first had sent him forth, lone over the wave, when he was an infant. Furthermore they set up by him a gold-wrought banner, high over his head; they let the holm bear him, gave him over to ocean; sad was their soul, mourning their mood. Men do not know to say of a sooth, not heads of Halls, men of mark under heaven, Who received that burthen!

Then was in the towers Beowulf of the Scyldings, the dear king of his people, for a long time famous among the nations—his father was gone other-where, patriarch from family seat—till in succession to him was born the lofty Healfdene; he governed while he lived, old and warlike, contended Scyldings. To him four children, one after another, awoke in the world: Heorogar commander of armies and Hroth-gar and Halga the good: I heard that Elan queen [of Ongentheow] was consort of the warlike Scylfing.

To Hrothgar was given martial spirit, warlike ambition; insomuch that his cousins gladly took him for leader, until the young generation grew up, a mighty regiment of clansmen. Into his mind it came, that he would give orders for men to construct a hall-building, a great mead-house, (greater) than the children of men had ever heard tell of; and that therewithin he would freely deal out to young and old what God should give him, save people's land and lives of men.

Then I heard of work widely proclaimed to many a tribe throughout this world, to make a fair gathering-place of people. His plan was in good time accomplished, with a quickness surprizing to men; so that it was all ready, the greatest of hall-buildings. He gave it the name of Heorot, he who with his word had wide dominion. He belied not his announcement;—rings he distributed, treasure at the banquet. The hall towered aloft, high and with pinnacles spanning the air; awaited the scathing blasts of destructive flame. No appearance was there as yet of knife-hatred starting up between son-in-law and father-in-law in revenge of blood.

Then the outcast creature, he who dwelt in darkness, with torture for a time endured that he heard joyance day by day, loud sounding in hall; there was the swough of the harp, the ringing song of the minstrel.

Said one who was skilled to narrate from remote time the primæval condition of men; quoth he— "The Almighty made the earth, the country radiant with beauty, all that water surroundeth, delighting in magnificence. He ordained Sun and Moon, luminaries for light to the dwellers on earth, and adorned the rustic regions with branches and leaves; life also he created for all the kinds that live and move."

Thus they, the warrior-band, in joyance lived and full delight;—until that one began to work atrocity, a fiend in the hall. The grim visitant was called Grendel, the dread mark-ranger, he who haunted moors, fen and fastness:—the unblessed man had long time kept the abode of monsters, ever since the Creator had proscribed them. On Cain's posterity did the eternal Lord wreak that slaughter, for that he slew Abel. He profited not by that violence; but He banished him far away, the Maker for that crime banished him from mankind. From that origin all strange broods awoke, eotens and elves and ogres, as well as giants who warred against God long time;— He repaid them due retribution.

He set out then as soon as night was come, to explore the lofty house; how the mailèd Danes had after carousal bestowed themselves in it. So he found therein a princely troop sleeping after feast; they knew not sorrow, desolation of men. The baleful wight, grim and greedy, was ready straight, fierce and furious, and in their sleep he seized thirty of the thanes; thence hied him back, yelling over his prey, to go to his home with the war-spoils, and reach his habitation. Then was in the dawning and with early day the war-craft of Grendel plain to the grooms; then was upraised after festivity the voice of weeping, a great cry in the morning. The illustrious ruler, the honoured prince, sat wobegone; majestic rage he tholed, he endured sorrow for his thanes:—since they had surveyed the track of the monster, of the accursed goblin;—that contest was too severe, horrible, and prolonged. It was not a longer space, but the interval of one night, that he again perpetrated a huger carnage; and he recked not of it—outrage and atrocity; he was too fixed in those things. Then was it not hard to find some who sought a resting-place elsewhere more at large, a bed among the castle-bowers, when to them was manifested and plainly declared by conspicuous proof that malice of the hellthane;—whoever had once escaped the fiend did from thenceforward hold himself farther aloof and closer. So domineered and nefariously warred he single against them all, until that the best of houses stood empty. The time was long; twelve winters' space did the Friend of the Scyldings suffer indignity, woes of every kind, unbounded sorrows; and so in process of time it became openly known to the sons of men through ballads in lamentable wise, that Grendel warred continually against Hrothgar; he waged malignant hostilities, violence and feud, many seasons, unremitting strife; he would not have peace with any man of the Danish power, or remove the life-bale, or compound for tribute; nor could any of the senators expect worthy compensation at the hands of the destroyer; the foul ruffian, a dark shadow of death, was pursuing the venerable and the youthful alike. He prowled about and lay in wait; at nights he continually held the misty moors;—men do not know in what direction hell's agents move in their rounds.

Many were the atrocities which the foe of mankind, the grisly prowler, oft accomplished, hard indignities,—Heorot he occupied, the richly decorated hall, in dark nights—yet he was by no means able to come nigh the throne, sacred to God, nor did he share the sentiment thereof.

That was a huge affliction for the friend of the Scyldings, heart breaking. Many a time and oft did the realm sit in conclave; they meditated on a remedy, what course it were best for them, soul-burthened men, to take against these awful horrors. Sometimes they vowed at idol fanes, honours of sacrifice; with words they prayed that the Goblin-queller would afford them relief against huge oppressions. Such was their custom, heathens' religion; they thought of hell in their imagination; they were not aware of the Maker, the Judge of actions, they knew not God the Governor, nor did they at all understand how to glorify the Crowned Head of the heavens, the Ruler of glory.

It is woe for him who is impelled by headlong perversity to plunge his soul into the gulph of fire; not to believe in consolation nor in any way turn:—well is it for him who is permitted, after death-day, to visit the Lord, and claim sanctuary in the Father's arms.

Thus was the son of Healfdene perpetually tossed with the trouble of that time; the sapient man was unable to avert the woe. Too heavy, horrible, and protracted was the struggle which had overtaken that people; tribulation cruel, hugest of nocturnal pests.

That in his distant home learnt a thane of Hygelac's, a brave man among the Goths; he learnt the deeds of Grendel; he was of mankind strongest in might in the day of this life; he was of noble birth and of robust growth. He ordered a wave-traveller, a good one, to be prepared for him; said he would pass over the swan-road and visit the gallant king, the illustrious ruler, inasmuch as he was in need of men. That adventure was little grudged him by sagacious men, though he was dear to them; they egged on the dareful spirit, they observed auguries. The brave man had selected champions of the Leeds of the Goths, the keenest whom he could find; with fourteen in company he took to ship;—a swain for pilot, a water-skilled man, pointed out the landmarks.

Time went on; the floater was on the waves, the boat under the cliff. Warriors ready dight mounted on the prow; currents eddied, surf against the beach; lads bore into the ship's lap bright apparel, gallant harness of war; the men, the brave men on adventure, shoved off the tight-timbered craft. So the foamy-necked floater went forth over the swelling ocean urged by the wind, most like to a bird; till that in due time, on the next day, the coily-stemmed cruiser had made such way that the voyagers saw land, sea-cliffs gleaming, hills towering, headlands stretching out to sea; then was the voyage accomplished, the water-passage ended. Then lightly up the Weder Leeds and sprang ashore, they made fast the sea-wood, they shook out their sarks, their war-weeds, they thanked God for that their seafaring had been easy.

Then from his rampart did the Scyldings' warden, he who had to guard the sea-cliffs, espy men bearing over bulwark bright shields, accoutrements ready for action;—curiosity urged him with impassioned thoughts (to learn) who those men were. Off he set then to the shore, riding on horseback, thane of Hrothgar; powerfully he brandished a huge lance in his hands, and he demanded with authoritative words—"Who are ye arm-bearing men, fenced with mail-coats, who have come thus with proud ship over the watery high-way, hither over the billows? Long time have I been in fort, stationed on the extremity of the country; I have kept the coast-guard, that on the land of the Danes no enemy with ship-harrying might be able to do hurt:—never have shield-bearing men more openly attempted to land here; nor do ye know beforehand the pass-word of our warriors, the confidential token of kinsmen. I never saw, of eorlas upon ground, a finer figure in harness that is one of yourselves; he is no mere goodman bedizened with armour, unless his look belies him, his unique aspect. Now I am bound to know your nationality, before ye on your way hence as explorers at large proceed any further into the land of the Danes. Now ye foreigners, mariners of the sea, ye hear my plain meaning; haste is best to let me know whence your comings are."

To him the chiefest gave answer; the captain of the band unlocked the treasure of words: "We are people of Gothic race, and hearth-fellow of Hygelac. My father was celebrated among the nations, a noble commander by the name of Ecgtheow; he lived to see many years, ere he departed an aged man out of his mansion; he is quickly remembered by every worshipful man all over the world. We with friendly intent have come to visit thy lord, the son of Healf-dene, the guardian of his people; be thou good to us with instructions! We have for the illustrious prince of the Danes a great message; there is no need to be dark about the matter, as I suppose. Thou knowest if it is so as we have heard say for a truth, that among the Scyldings some strange depredator, a mysterious author of deeds, in the darkness of night inflicts in horrible wise monstrous atrocy, indignity, and havoc. Of this I can, in all sincerity of heart, teach Hrothgar a remedy; how he, so wise and good, shall overpower the enemy; if for him the fight of afflic-tions was ever destined to take a turn, better times to come again, and the seethings of anguish grow calmer; or else for ever hereafter tholeth he a time of tribulation, sore distress, so long as the best of houses resteth there upon her eminence."

The Warden addressed them, where he sat on his horse, an officer undaunted: "Of every particular must a sharp esquire know the certainty as to words and words—any one who hath a sense of duty. I gather from what I hear that this is a friendly band to the lord of the Scyldings. March ye forward bear-ing weapons and weeds, I will guide you: likewise I will command my kinsmen thanes to honourably to keep against every foe your vessel, the newly dight, the boat on the beach: until the neck-laced craft shall bear back again over the water-streams her dear lord to Wedermark. To such a benign adventurer is it given, that he passeth unscathed through the encounter of battle."

They proceeded then on their march; the vessel remained still, rode on her cable, the wide-bosomed ship, at anchor fast;—the boar-figures shone, over the cheek-guards, prankt with gold, ornate and hard-welded;—the farrow kept guard. In fighting mood they raged along, the men pushed forward; down-hill they ran together, until they could see the Hall structure, gallant and gold-adorned; that was to dwellers on earth the most celebrated of all mansions under the sky, that in which the Ruler dwelt; the gleam of it shot over many lands. Then did the warrior point out to them the court of the valiant, which was now conspicuous;—that they could go straight to it. Like a man of war, he wheeled about his horse, and spake a parting word; "It is time for me to go; may the allwielding Father graciously keep you safe in adventures! I will to the sea, to keep guard against hostile force."

The street was stone-paven; the path guided the banded men. The war-corslet shone, hard, hand-locked; the polished ring-iron sang in its meshes, when they in grim harness now came marching to the Hall. The sea-weary men set down their broad shields, bucklers mortal hard, against the terrace of that mansion. Then they seated themselves on the bench;—their mail-coats rang, harness of warriors;—the spears stood, sea-men's artillery, stacked together, ash-timber with tip of grey; the iron troop was accoutred worthily.

Then a proud officer there questioned the martial crew as to their kindred:—"Whence bring ye damasked shields, grey sarks, and visored helms;—a pile of war shafts? I am Hrothgar's herald and esquire. Never saw I foreigners, so many men, loftier looking. I think that ye for daring, not at all of desperate fortune, but for courageous emprize, have come to visit Hrothgar."

To him then with gallant bearing answered the proud leed of the Wederas; words spake he back, firm under helmet:—"We are Hygelac's table-fellows; my name is Beowulf. I will expound mine errand to the son of Healfdene, to the illustrious prince, to thy lord, if he will deign us that we may approach him so good."

Wulfgar addressed them—that was a leed of the Wendlas; his courage had been witnessed by many, his valour and wisdom:—"Thereanent will I ask the Friend of the Danes, the Scyldings' lord, the ring-dispenser, according as thou dost petition, the illustrious chief (will I ask) concerning thy visit; and to thee promptly declare the answer, which the brave prince is pleased to give me."

Thereupon he returned briskly to where Hrothgar sate, old and hoary, with his guard of warriors: he went with gallant bearing till he took his stand before the shoulders of the Danish prince; he knew the custom of nobility. Wulfgar addressed himself to his liege lord: "Here are arrived, come from far, over the circuit of ocean, men of the Goths; the companions name their chief Beowulf. They make petition, that they, my prince, may be permitted to exchange discourse with thee: do not thou award them a refusal of thy conversation, benignant Hrothgar! They by their war-harness appear worthy of the reverence of eorlas; certainly the chief is a valiant man, he who has conducted those martial comrades hither."

Hrothgar, crown of Scyldings, uttered speech; "I knew him when he was a page. His good old father was Ecgtheow by name; to whose home Hrethel of the Goths gave over his only daughter; it is of his off-spring surely, his grown-up son, that is hither come, come to visit a loyal friend. Sure enough they did say that—the sailors who carried thither for compliment the presents to the Goths—that he hath thirty men's strength in his handgrip, a valiant campaigner. Him hath holy God of high grace sent to us, sent to the western Danes, as I hope, against Grendel's terror; I must proffer the brave man treasures for his greatheartedness. Be thou full of alacrity, request the banded friends to enter, one and all, into my presence. Say to them moreover expressly with words, that they are welcome visitors to the Danish leeds." [Then to the door of the hall Wulfgar went] he announced his message:—"To you I am commanded to say by my chieftain the lord of the eastern Danes, that he knoweth your noble ancestry, and ye to him are, over the sea-waves, men of hardihood, welcome hither. Now ye can go, in your warlike equipage, with helm on head, to the presence of Hrothgar; leave the war-boards, here to abide, and the wooden battle-shafts till the parley is over." Up then arose the prince: about him many a trooper, a splendid band of thanes; some remained there, they kept the armour, as their brave captain bade. They formed all together, as the officer (Wulfgar) showed the way, under the roof of Heorot; [he went with courage high] with a firm look under his helmet, till he took his stand in the royal chamber. Beowulf uttered a speech—on him his byrnie shone, a curious net-work linked by cunning device of the artificer—"To Hrothgar hail!

I am Hygelac's kinsman and cousin-thane; I have undertaken many exploits in youngsterhood. To me on
my native soil the affair of Grendel became openly
known; seafaring men say that this hall do stand, fab-
ric superb, of every trooper empty and useless, as
soon as the light of evening under the cope of
heaven is hidden from view. Then did my people, the
best of them, sagacious fellows, O royal Hrothgar, in-
sense me that I should visit thee; because they knew
the strength of my might; they had themselves been
spectators when I came off my campaign battered by
foes, where I bound five monsters, humbled the
eoten brood; and in the waves I slew nickers in the
night-time, I ran narrow risks, avenged the grievance
of the Wederas—they had been acquainted with
grief—a grinding I gave the spoilers;—and now
against Grendel I am bound, against that formidable
one, single-handed, to champion the quarrel against
the giant. Wherefore I will now petition thee, prince
of the glorious Danes, thou roof-tree of the Scyldings, one petition; that thou refuse me not, oh thou
shelter of warriors, thou imperial lord of nations,
now I have come from such a distance, that I may
have the task alone—I and my band of eorls, this
knot of hardy men—to purge Heorot. I have learnt
too that the terrible one out of bravado despises
weapons; I therefore will forgo the same—as I hope
that Hygelac my prince may be to me of mood

benignant,—that I bear not sword or broad shield, or yellow buckler, to the contest; but with handgrip I undertake to encounter the enemy, and contend for life, foe to foe; there shall he whom death taketh resign himself to the doom of the Lord.

"I suppose that he will, if he can have his way, in the hall of battle devour fearlessly the man of the Goths, just as he often did the power of the Hrethmen. Thou wilt not need to cover my head (with a mound), but he will have me all blood-besprent, if death taketh me; he will bear away the gory corpse with intent to feast upon it, the solitary ranger will eat it remorselessly, will stain the moor-swamps; no need wilt thou have to care any longer for the disposal of my body. Send to Hygelac, if Hild take me, the matchless armour that protects my breast, bravest of jackets;—that is a relic of Hrethla's, a work of Wéland's. Wyrd goeth ever as she is bound."

Hrothgar, crown of Scyldings, uttered speech: "For pledgèd rescue thou, Beowulf my friend, and at honour's call, hast come to visit us. Thy father did fight out a mighty feud; he was the banesman of Heatholaf among the Wylfings; then the nation could not keep him for dread of invasion. Therefrom he went over the yeasty waves to visit the

Southron folk of the Danes, of the honourable Scyldings, at the time when I had just then become king over the Danish folk, and in my prime swayed the jewel-stored treasure-city of heroes: when Heregar my elder brother was dead, no longer living, Halfdene's son. He was better than I! Afterwards I composed the feud for money; I sent to the Wylfings over the water's ridge ancient treasures; he swore oaths (of homage) to me.

"It is a sorrow for me in my soul to tell to any mortal man what humiliation, what horrors, Grendel hath brought upon me in Heorot with his malignant stratagems. My hall-troop, my warrior band, is reduced to nothing; Wyrd hath swept them away in the hideous visitation of Grendel. God unquestionably can arrest the fell destroyer in his doings. Full oft they boasted when refreshed with beer, troop-fellows over the ale-can, that they in the beer-hall would receive Grendel's onset with clash of swords. Then was this mead-hall at morning-tide, this royal saloon bespattered with gore, at blush of dawn, all the bench-timber was reeking with blood, the hall with deadly gore; so much the less owned I of trusty lieges, of dear nobility, when death had taken those away.

"Sit now to banquet, and merrily share the feast, brave captain, with (thy) fellows, as thy mind moves thee."

Then was there for the Goth-men all together, in the beer-hall, a table cleared; there the resolute men went to sit in the pride of their strength. A thane attended to the service; one who bore in his hand a decorated ale-can; he poured forth the sheer nectar. At times a minstrel sang, clear-voiced in Heorot; there was social merriment, a brave company of Danes and Wederas.

Unferth made a speech, Ecglaf's son; he who sate at the feet of the Scyldings' lord, broached a quarrelsome theme—the adventure of Beowulf the high-souled voyager was great despite to him, because he grudged that any other man should ever in the world achieve more exploits under heaven than he himself:—"Art thou that Beowulf, he who strove with Breca on open sea in swimming-match, where ye twain out of bravado explored the floods, and foolhardily in deep water jeoparded your lives? nor could any man, friend or foe, turn the pair of you from the dismal adventure! What time ye twain plied in swimming, where ye twain covered with your arms the awful stream, meted the sea-streets, buffeted with hands, shot over ocean; the deep boiled with waves, a wintry surge. Ye twain in the realm of waters toiled a se'nnight; he at swimming outvied thee, had greater force. Then in morning hour the swell cast him ashore on the Heathoram people, whence he made for his own patrimony, dear to his Leeds he made for the land of the Brondings, a fair stronghold, where he was lord of folk, of city, and of rings. All his boast to thee-ward, Beanstan's son smoothly fulfilled. Wherefore I anticipate for thee worse luck—though thou wert everywhere doughty in battle-shocks, in grim war-tug—if though darest bide in Grendel's way a night-long space."

Beowulf son of Ecgtheow uttered speech:— "Lo, big things hast thou, my friend Unferth, beer-exalted, spoken about Breca; hast talked of his adventure! Rightly I claim, that I have proved more sea-power, more buffetings in waves, than any other man. He and I used to talk when we were pages, and we used to brag of thism we were both of us at that time in youngsterhood—how that we two would out on the main and put our lives in jeopardy; and that we matched so. Drawn sword we had, as we at swimming plied, firm in hand: we meant to guard us against the whale-fishes. Not a whit from me could he further fleet on sea-waves, swifter on holm; not from him would I. So we twain kept together in the sea for the space of five nights, till the flood parted us, the seething billows, coldest weather, darkening night, and a fierce wind from the north came dead against us; rough were the waves. The sea-fishes' temper was stirred; and then it was that my body-sark, firm, hand-locked, gave me help against the spiteful ones; the plaited war-jacket lay about my breast, gold-pranked. Me to bottom dragged a spotty monster, tight the grim thing had me in grip; nathless 'twas given me that I got at the vermin with point, with hand-bill; combat dispatched the mighty sea-brute by my hand."

"As repeatedly as the spiteful assailants shrewdly pressed me, I served them (liberally) with precious sword as was meet. They did not have their slaughter-ous revel, the foul brigands, that they should eat me up sitting around their supper, by the floor of the sea; but (on the contrary) next morning, wounded with weapons along the wrack of the wave, they lay high and dry; by swords they had their quietus, so that never afterwards about the swelling highway should they let seafaring men of their destined course.

"Light came from the East, the bright signal of God; the waves grew calm, so that I was able to see the forelands, the windy walls. Fortune often rescues the warrior, if he is not fated to die; provided that his courage is sound! Anyhow 'twas my good luck, that I slew with the sword nine nicors. Never did I hear of a harder fight under heaven's roof in the night-time, nor of a man more distressed in ocean streams; howbeit I escaped the clutch of foes with my life, though worn and spent. Me the sea upcast, the swirling flood, upon the land of the Fins, the heaving billow. I never heard say aught by thee of such deadly fightings, sword-clashings: Breca never yet, at war play, not he nor you, deed achieved so valorously with flashing swords—of that I brag not much—though thou wast banesman to thy brother, thy next of kin; for which thou shalt in hell damnation dree, though doughty be thy wit. I say to thee of a sooth, thou son of Ecglaf, that never had Grendel the foul ruffian made such a tale of horrors for thy prince, such disgrace in Heorot, if thy courage were, if thy spirit were, so formidable as thou thyself claimest. But he hath found out that he need not greatly fear reprisals, grisly edge-clash, from your people, the mighty Scyldings; he taketh blackmail, respecteth no one of the people of the Danes, but maketh a sport of war, slaughtereth and feasteth:—no thought hath he of a fight with the spear-Danes. But now shall the Goth show him erelong puissance and emprize in the way of war. After that, he who can shall go proud into the mead-hall, when over the sons of men the morning light of another day, the sun, with radiance clothed, shall shine from the south."

Then was in bliss the dispenser of wealth, greyhaired and militant; he believed in help; the prince of the glorious Danes, the shepherd of the people, perceived in Beowulf a resolute purpose. There was laughter of mighty men; music sounded; the words (of song) were jovial.

Wealhtheow moved forward, Hrothgar's queen, mindful of ceremonies; she greeted in her gold array the men in Hall; and then the noble lady presented the beaker first to the sovereign of the east-Danes, wished him blithe at the banquet, and dear to his Leeds;—he merrily enjoyed the feast and the Hall-cup, valiant king. Then the Helming princess went the round, to elder and to younger, every part; handed the jewelled cup; till the moment came, that she, the diademed queen, with dignity befitting, brought the mead-cup nigh to Beowulf; she greeted the Leed of the Goths, she thanked God with wise choice of words, for that her desire was come to pass, that she in any warrior believed for remedy of woes. He, the death-doing warrior, accepted the beaker at Wealhtheow's hand, and then he descanted, elate for battle;—Beowulf son of Ecgtheow uttered speech: "I undertook that, when I went on board, and sate on the sea-boat, with the company of my fellows, that I once for all would work out the will of your Leeds, or fall in the death-struggle, in the grip of the fiend. I am bound as an eorl to fulfil the emprize, or in this mead-hall to meet my death-day." To the lady the words were well-liking, the vaunt-speech of the Goth; she walked gold-arrayed, high-born queen of the nation, to sit by her lord.

Then was again as erst within the hall the lofty word outspoken, the company was happy, the sound was that of a mighty people; until that sudden the son of Healfdene was minded to retire to his nightly rest; he knew that against the high Hall war was determined by the monster, from the time when they could [not] see the sun's light or shrouding night came over all, and the creatures of darkness came stalking abroad; he warred in obscurity. All the company arose. Then did man greet man, Hrothgar greeted Beowulf, bespake him luck, mastery in the house of hospitality; and delivered this speech: "Never before, since I could heave hand and shield, did I confide the guard-house of the Danes to any man, but only to thee now on this occasion. Have now and hold the best of houses; resolve on success: show valour amain; be vigilant against the foe! Thou shalt not have any desire unfulfilled, if thou that mighty work with life achievest."

So Hrothgar, chief of Scyldings, took his departure with retinue of men, out of hall; he was minded to join Wealhtheow his queen and consort.

The Glory of kings had—so men told one another—set up a hall-warden against Grendel; he had
undertaken the single service about the patriarch
of the Danes, offered watch against the monster;—
assuredly the Gothic Leed with joyous mien trusted
in valorous might and the smile of Providence.

Then put he off from him his iron byrnie, helmet
from head; delivered to his esquire the richly-dight
sword, choicest steel; and charged him with the care
of his war-harness. Then did the valiant man Beowulf the Goth utter some vaunting words ere he
mounted on bed: "I reckon myself to be in the fury
of battle, in warlike feats, no wise below the preten-
sions of Grendel; for that reason I will not with
sword give him his quietus, deprive him of life, although I very well may. Nought knoweth he of
those gentle practices, to give and take sword-cuts,
to hew the shield; dread though he be in feats of
horror—but we twain shall in the night-time su-
persede the blade, if he dare to court war without
weapon; and thereafter may the Allwise God, the
holy Lord, adjudge success on which side soever
may to him appear meet!"

Then the daring warrior laid him down; the pil-
low received the countenance of the eorl; and
round about him many a smart sea-warrior
couched to his hall-rest. Not one of them thought
that from that place he should ever again visit his

own estate, his folk and castle, where he was brought up, but they had been informed that before now a bloody death had all too much reduced them, the Danish people, in that festive hall. But to them, the Leeds of Wedermark, did the Lord grant webs of war-speed, strength and support, that they by the force of one, by his single prowess, should all be victorious over their foe. For a truth it is shewn, that the mighty God has governed mankind in every age!

He came in dim night, marching along, ranger of the dark. The defenders slept, they whose duty it was to guard that gabled mansion—all slept but one!

It was very well known to all men, that the ruthless destroyer might not against the will of God whirl them under darkness; but (all the same) he, vigilant in defiance of the foe, awaited in fullfraught mood the arbitrament of battle.

Then came Grendel marching from the moor under the misty brows; he bore the wrath of God. The assassin meant to catch some one of humankind in that lofty hall; he tore along under heaven in the direction where he knew the hospitable building, the gold-hall of men, metal-spangled, ever ready for his entertainment;—that was not the first time he had visited Hrothgar's homestead. Never had he in his life-days, earlier or later, met so tough a warrior, such hall-guards!

Came then journeying to the hall the felon mirth-bereft; suddenly the door, fastened with bars of wrought iron, sprang open as soon as he touched it with his hands; thus bale-minded and big with rage he wrecked the vestibule of the hall. Quickly after that the fiend was treading on the paven floor; he went ravening; out of his eyes there stood likest to flame an eerie light. He perceived in the hall many warriors, a troop of kinsmen, grouped together, a band of cousins, asleep. Then was his mood exalted to laughter; he counted, the fell ruffian, that he should sever, ere day came, the life of each one of them from his body, seeing that luck had favoured him to gratify his slaughterous appetite. That was not however so destined, that he should be permitted to eat any more of mankind after that night.

Mighty rage the kinsman of Hygelac curbed, considering how the assassin meant to proceed in the course of his ravenings. Nor was the marauder minded to delay it; but he seized promptly at his first move a sleeping warrior, tore him in a moment, crunched the bony frame, drank blood of veins, swallowed huge morsels; in a trice he had devoured the lifeless body, feet, hands, and all. He stepped up nearer forward; he was then taking with his hand the great-hearted warrior on his bed. The fiend reached towards him with his fang;—he promptly seized with shrewd design and grappled his arm. Quickly did the boss of horrors discover that, that never in all the world, all the quarters of the earth, had he met man more strange with bigger hand-grip; he in mood became alarmed in spirit; but never the quicker could he get away. His mind was to be going; he wanted to flee into darkness; rejoin the devils' pack; his entertainment there was not such as before he had met with in bygone days. Then did the brave kinsman of Hygelac remember his discourse of the evening; up he stood full length, and grappled with him amain; his fingers cracked as they would burst. The monster was making off, the eorl followed him up. The oaf was minded, if so be he might, to fling himself loose, and away therefrom to flee into fen-hollows; he knew that the control of his fingers was in the grip of a terrible foe; that was a rash expedition which the devastator had made to Heorot!

The Guard-hall roared;—upon all the Danes, upon the inhabiters of the castle, upon every brave man, upon the eorlas, came moral panic. Furious were both the maddened champions, the building resounded; it was a great wonder that the genial saloon endured the combatants, that it did not fall to ground, that fair ornament of the country; only that it was inwardly and outwardly so firmly besmithied with iron staunchions of masterly skill! There, from the still started—as my story tells—many a mead-bench adorned with gold, where the terrible ones contended. Thereanent had the Scylding senators weened at the first, that never would any man by mortal force be able to wreck it, the beautiful and ivoried house, or by craft to disjoint it;—leastwise fire's embrace should swallow it up in vapoury reek.

The noise rose high, with renewed violence; the north-Danes were stricken with eldritch horror every one, whosoever heard even out on the wall the doleful cry, the adversary of God yelling a dismal lay, a song unvictorious:—the thral of hell howling for his wound. He held him too fast, he who was in main the strongest of men in the day of this life.

The shelter of eorlas was not by any means minded to let the murderous visitant escape alive; he did not reckon his life-days useful to any one of the Leeds. There did many an eorl of Beowulf's unsheath his old heirloom;—would rescue the life of their master, their great captain; if so be they might. They knew it not,—when they plunged into the fight, the stouthearted companions, and thought to hack him on every side, reach his life,—that no choicest blade upon earth, no war-bill would touch that destroyer, but he had by enchantment secured himself against victorious weapons, edges of all kinds. His life-parting [in the day of this life] was destined to be woeful, and the outcast spirit must travel far off into the realm of fiends. Then discovered he that, he who erst in wanton mood had wrought huge atrocity upon mankind—he was out of God's peace—that his body was not at his command, but the valiant kinsman of Hygelac had got hold of him by the hand; to either was the other's life loathsome. A deadly wound the foul warlock got; on his shoulder the fatal crack appeared; the sinews sprang wide, the bone-coverings burst. To Beowulf was victory given; Grendel must flee life-sick therefrom to the coverts of the fen, must make for a cheerless habitation;—full well he knew that the end of his life was reached, the number of his days. All the Danes had in the issue of that dire struggle the fulfilment of their desire.

He had then purged, he who but now came from far, sagacious and resolute, Hrothgar's hall; he had rescued it from danger; had succeeded in his night-task with brilliant achievement. The Leed of the Gothic companions had made good his vaunt to the east-Danes; likewise he had entirely remedied the horror, the harrowing sorrow, which they were enduring before, and of dire necessity were forced to

suffer;—huge indignity. That was a token conspicuous, when the hero of battle had affixed the hand,
arm, and shoulder—that was the whole affair of
Grendel's fang—under the gabled roof.

Then was in the morning—so goes my story—
about the gift-hall many a warrior; the chiefs of the
folk came from far and near, through divers ways, to
survey the prodigy, the traces of the loathed one. His
life-ending was no grief whatever to any of those
who surveyed the track of the vanquished, how he
in doleful mood away from that place, in buffets
worsted; had, death-doomed and fugitive, fled in
mortal terror to the Nicers' mere. There was the
face of the lake surging with blood, the gruesome
plash of waves all turbid with reeking gore, with
sword-spilth;—presently he, void of joyance, in
fenny covert yielded up his life, his heathen soul;
there did Hela receive him.

Thence back home went the old Companions
along with many a bachelor from the pleasure-trip;
from the Mere in high spirits riding on horses,
barons on jennets. There was Beowulf's achievement rehearsed; many a one often said that south
nor north between the seas all the wide world over,

other none of shield-bearing warriors under the compass of the firmament preferable were or worthier of sovereignty. They did not however at all disparage their natural lord, gracious Hrothgar; but he was a good King!

Now and then the gallant warriors loosened their russet nags for a gallop, to run a match, where the turfways looked fair, or were favorably known. Otherwhiles a thane of the king's, bombastic groom, his mind full of ballads, the man who remembered good store of old-world tales—word followed word by the bond of truth—began anon to rehearse, cunningly to compose, the adventure of Beowulf, and fluently to pursue the story in its order, with interlacing words. At large he detailed, what he had heard say of Sigemund's exploits, much that was strange, the battle-toil of the Wælsing, distant expeditions, things the sons of men quite knew not of, feud and atrocity;—none but Fitela by his side, when he would say aught of such matter, uncle to nephew, as they had ever stood by one another in every struggle: they had with swords laid low many of the monster brood. To Sigemund there sprang up after his death-day no little fame; forasmuch as he, hardy in fight, had quelled the Dragon, the keeper of treasure; he, the son of a prince, in under the hoary rock, single-handed enterprized the perilous deed;—Fitela was not with him. Nathless he succeeded so

well that the sword sped through the stupendous
worm, till it struck in the bank, noble iron! the
dragon died the death. The champion had by valour
attained that he might enjoy the jewel-hoard at his
own discretion; he laded the sea-boat, the son of
Wæls bore to the bosom of the ship the bright ornaments; the Worm dissolved with heat. He was by
daring exploits the most famous of adventurers far
and wide over the world, shelter of warriors; such
eminence he won.

When Heremod's warfare had slackened, his puissance and emprize, he among the Eotens was de-
coyed forth into the power of enemies, promptly
sent out of the way. Him did billows of sorrow dis-
able too long; he to his Leeds, to all his princes, became a loyal anxiety. Moreover, in his earlier times,
many a wise countryman had often deplored the
adventurous life of the ardent soul, such a one as had
trusted to him for remedy of grievances, that the
royal child might grow powerful, succeed to the
state of his fathers, protect the people, the treasure
and the castle, realm of heroes, patrimony of the
Scyldings. There was he, Hygelac's kinsman, to all
mankind, and to his friends, more acceptable; the
other was seized with fury.

At intervals racing they with their horses measured the fallow streets. Then was the light of morning launched and advanced; there was many a varlet

going eager-minded to the lofty Hall to see the strange prodigy;—likewise the king himself from his domestic lodge, keeper of jewelled hoards, trod with glorious mien, gorgeously distinguished in the midst of a great retinue;—and his queen with him, measured the path to the mead-hall with a bevy of ladies.

Hrothgar uttered speech—he was going to Hall; he stood on the Staple; he beheld the steep roof gold-glittering, and the hand of Grendel.

"For this spectacle a thanksgiving to the almighty be done without delay! Much despite I endured, capturings by Grendel; always can God work wonder after wonder, the Lord of Glory! It was but now that I thought I should never see a remedy for any of my woes, while the best of houses stood bloodstained, soaked in slaughter; the woe had scattered all my senators, as men who weened not that they ever should rescue the national edifice of my Leeds from the hateful ones, the demons and bogles.

"Now hath a lad, through might of God, achieved the deed which we all erewhile were unable with our wisdom to compass. Lo! that may she say, what lady soever mothered that child by human generation, if yet she liveth, that to her was the Ancient Master favourable in her child-bearing!

"Now I will heartily love thee, Beowulf, youth most excellent, as if thou wert my son; from this time forth keep thou up the new relation. There shall be no lack to thee of any desires in the world, so far as I have power. Full oft have I for less service decreed recompense, honour from the treasury, to a less distinguished hero, less prompt to fight.

"Thou thyself hast by deeds achieved, that thy fame will live ever and always. May the Almighty reward thee with good, as he hath just now done!"

Beowulf uttered speech, Ecgtheow's son: "We discharged that high task, fighting with right good heart; shrewdly we enterprized the terror of the unknown. I'd a liked it vastly better, that thou'dst a seen his very self, the fiend in full gear, ready to drop. I thought quickly to fix him on a bloody bed with hard grapplings, that he for my hand-grip should lie death-struggling, unless his body vanished; I could not, as the Ancient would not, baulk his passage; I did not stick close enough to him, the man-queller; the fiend was too over-mighty in his making off. However he left his fist—to save his life and mark his track—his arm and shoulder: not thereby however has the wretched being bought reprieve; none the longer will he live, the loathsome pest burthened with crimes; but the wound hath him, in deadly grip close pinioned, in baleful bands; in that condition must he, crime-stained wretch, abide the great doom, according as the Ancient One may will to assign his portion."

A silenter man was then the son of Ecglaf in the brag of martial exploits; since it was by the hero's valour the ethelings beheld the hand, the fiendish fingers, over the high roof, every one straight before him. Each one of the nail-places was likest to steel, hand-spur of the heathenish marauder, horrible spikes; every one declared there was nothing so hard would graze them, no sword of old celebrity that would take off the monster's bloody war-fist.

Then was order promptly given that the interior of Heorot should be decorated; many they were, of men and of women, who garnished that genial palace, hospitable hall. Gold-glittering shone the brocaded tapestries along the walls, pictures many for the wonder of all people who have an eye for such. That bright building was terribly wrecked in its whole interior, though it had been strengthened with iron fastenings; the hinged were wrenched away; the roof alone had escaped altogether unhurt, when the destroyer, stained with atrocities, took to flight in desperation of life.

It is not easy to elude [death], try it who will; but every living soul of the sons of men, of dwellers upon ground, must of necessity approach the destined spot, where his body, bedded in fast repose, shall sleep after supper.

Then was the time and the moment, that Healfdene's son should go to Hall; the king was minded himself to share the feast. Never that I heard of did that nation in stronger force about their bounty-giver more bravely muster. They went to bench in merry guise—while their kinsmen enjoyed the copious feast, and with fair courtesy quaffed many a mead-bowl—mighty men in the lofty hall, Hrothgar and Hrothulf. The interior of Heorot was wholly filled with friends; no treachery had imperial Scyldings at that early date attempted.

Then did the son of Healfdene present to Beowulf a golden ensign in reward of victory, decorated staff-banner, helmet and mail-coat; many beheld when they brought the grand treasure-sword before the hero. Beowulf tasted the beaker on the hall-floor; no need had he to be ashamed of that bounty-giving before the archers. I heard not many instances of men giving to other at ale-bench four treasures gold-bedight in friendlier wise. About the helmet's roof the crest was fastened with wire-bound fencing for the head, in order that file-wrought war-scoured blades might not cruelly scathe it, when the shielded fighter had to go against angry foes.

Then did the Shelter of eorlas command to bring eight horses gold-cheeked into the court within the palings; on one of them stood the saddle gaily caparisoned and decorated with silver, which was the war-seat of the high king, when the son of Healf-dene was minded to exercise the play of swords;— never failed in the front the charger of the famous (king) when the slain were falling. And then did the chief of the Ingwines deliver unto Beowulf possession of both at once, both horses and arms;—bade him enjoy them well. So manfully did the illustri-ous chieftain, the hoard-warden of heroes, reward battle-risks with horses and treasures, so as never will any mispraise them who is minded to speak sooth according to right.

Robin Hood

[**HOWARD PYLE**]

I n merry England in the time of old, when
good King Henry the Second ruled the land,
there lived within the green glades of Sherwood Forest, near Nottingham Town, a famous outlaw whose name was Robin Hood. No archer ever
lived that could speed a gray goose shaft with such
skill and cunning as his, nor were there ever such
yeomen as the sevenscore merry men that roamed
with him through the greenwood shades. Right
merrily they dwelt within the depths of Sherwood
Forest, suffering neither care nor want, but passing
the time in merry games of archery or bouts of
cudgel play, living upon the King's venison, washed
down with draughts of ale of October brewing.

Not only Robin himself but all the band were
outlaws and dwelt apart from other men, yet they

were beloved by the country people round about, for no one ever came to jolly Robin for help in time of need and went away again with an empty fist.

And now I will tell how it first came about that Robin Hood fell afoul of the law.

When Robin was a youth of eighteen, stout of sinew and bold of heart, the Sheriff of Nottingham proclaimed a shooting-match and offered a prize of a butt of ale to whomsoever should shoot the best shaft in Nottinghamshire. "Now," quoth Robin, "will I go too, for fain would I draw a string for the bright eyes of my lass, and a butt of good October brewing." So up he got and took his good stout yew bow and a score or more of broad clothyard arrows, and started off from Locksley Town through Sherwood Forest to Nottingham.

It was at the dawn of day in the merry May-time, when hedgerows are green and flowers bedeck the meadows; daisies pied and yellow cuckoo buds and fair primroses all along the briery hedges; when apple buds blossom and sweet birds sing, the lark at dawn of day, the throstle cock and cuckoo; when lads and lasses look upon each other with sweet thoughts; when busy housewives spread their linen to bleach upon the bright green grass. Sweet was the greenwood as he walked along its paths, and bright the green and rustling leaves, amid which the little birds sang with might and main: and blithely

Robin whistled as he trudged along, thinking of Maid Marian and her bright eyes, for at such times a youth's thoughts are wont to turn pleasantly upon the lass that he loves the best.

As thus he walked along with a brisk step and merry whistle, he came suddenly upon some foresters seated beneath a great oak tree. Fifteen there were in all, making themselves merry with feasting and drinking as they sat around a huge pasty, to which each man helped himself, thrusting his hands into the pie, and washing down that which they ate with great horns of ale which they drew all foaming from a barrel that stood nigh. Each man was clad in Lincoln green, and a fine show they made, seated upon the sward beneath that fair, spreading tree. Then one of them, with his mouth full, called out to Robin,—

"Hulloa, where goest thou, little lad, with thy one penny bow and thy farthing shafts?"

Then Robin grew angry, for no stripling likes to be taunted with his green years.

"Now," quoth he, "my bow and eke mine arrows are as good as thine; and moreover, I go to the shooting-match at Nottingham Town, which same has been proclaimed by our good Sheriff of Nottinghamshire; there I will shoot with other stout yeomen, for a prize has been offered of a fine butt of ale."

Then one who held a horn of ale in his hand, said, "Ho! listen to the lad! Why, boy, thy mother's milk is yet scarce dry upon thy lips, and yet thou pratest of standing up with good stout men at Nottingham butts, thou who art scarce able to draw one string of a two stone bow."

"I'll hold the best of you twenty marks," quoth bold Robin, "that I hit the clout at threescore rods, by the good help of Our Lady fair."

At this all laughed aloud, and one said, "Well boasted, thou fair infant, well boasted! and well thou knowest that no target is nigh to make good thy wager."

And another cried, "He will be taking ale with his milk next."

At this Robin grew right mad. "Hark ye," said he; "yonder, at the glade's end, I see a herd of deer, even more than threescore rods distant. I'll hold you twenty marks that, by leave of Our Lady, I cause the best hart among them to die."

"Now done!" cried he who had spoken first. "And here are twenty marks. I wager that thou causest no beast to die, with or without the aid of Our Lady."

Then Robin took his good yew bow in his hand, and placing the tip at his instep, he strung it right deftly; then he nocked a broad clothyard arrow, and, raising the bow, drew the gray goose-feather to his ear; the next moment the bow-string rang and the arrow sped down the glade as a sparrowhawk skims in a northern wind. High leaped the noblest hart of all the herd, only to fall dead, reddening the green path with his heart's blood.

"Ha!" cried Robin, "how likest thou that shot, good fellow? I wot the wager were mine, an it were three hundred pounds."

Then all the foresters were filled with rage, and he who had spoken the first and had lost the wager was more angry than all.

"Nay," cried he, "the wager is none of thine, and get thee gone, straightway, or, by all the saints of heaven, I'll baste thy sides until thou wilt ne'er be able to walk again."

"Knowest thou not," said another, "that thou hast killed the King's deer, and, by the laws of our gracious lord and sovereign, King Harry, thine ears should be shaven close to thy head?"

"Catch him!" cried a third.

"Nay," said a fourth, "let him e'en go because of his tender years."

Never a word said Robin Hood, but he looked at the foresters with a grim face; then, turning on his heel, strode away from them down the forest glade. But his heart was bitterly angry, for his blood was hot and youthful and prone to boil.

Now, well would it have been for him who had first spoken had he left Robin Hood alone; but his anger was hot, both because the youth had gotten the better of him and because of the deep draughts of ale that he had been quaffing. So, of a sudden, without any warning, he sprang to his feet, and seized upon his bow and fitted it to a shaft. "Ay," cried he, "and I'll hurry thee anon;" and he sent the arrow whistling after Robin.

It was well for Robin Hood that that same forester's head was spinning with ale, or else he would never have taken another step; as it was, the arrow whistled within three inches of his head. Then he turned around and quickly drew his own bow, and sent an arrow back in return.

"Ye said I was no archer," cried he aloud, "but say so now again!"

The shaft flew straight; the archer fell forward with a cry, and lay on his face upon the ground, his arrows rattling about him from out of his quiver, the gray goose shaft wet with his heart's blood. Then, before the others could gather their wits about them, Robin Hood was gone into the depths of the greenwood. Some started after him, but not with much heart, for each feared to suffer the death of his fellow; so presently they all came and lifted the dead man up and bore him away to Nottingham Town.

Meanwhile Robin Hood ran through the greenwood. Gone was all the joy and brightness from everything, for his heart was sick within him, and it was borne in upon his soul that he had slain a man.

"Alas!" cried he, "thou hast found me an archer that will make thy wife to wring! I would that thou hadst ne'er said one word to me, or that I had never passed thy way, or e'en that my right forefinger had been stricken off ere that this had happened! In haste I smote, but grieve I sore at leisure!" And then, even in his trouble, he remembered the old saw that "What is done is done; and the egg cracked cannot be cured."

And so he came to dwell in the greenwood that was to be his home for many a year to come, never again to see the happy days with the lads and lasses of sweet Locksley Town; for he was outlawed, not only because he had killed a man, but also because he had poached upon the King's deer, and two hundred pounds were set upon his head, as a reward for whoever would bring him to the court of the King.

Now the Sheriff of Nottingham swore that he himself would bring this knave, Robin Hood, to justice, and for two reasons: first, because he wanted the two hundred pounds, and next, because the forester that Robin Hood had killed was of kin to him.

But Robin Hood lay hidden in Sherwood Forest for one year, and in that time there gathered around him many others like himself, cast out from other folk for this cause and for that. Some had shot deer in hungry winter time, when they could get no other food, and had been seen in the act by the foresters, but had escaped, thus saving their ears; some had been turned out of their inheritance, that their farms might be added to the King's lands in Sherwood Forest; some had been despoiled by a great baron or a rich abbot or a powerful esquire,— all, for one cause or another, had come to Sherwood to escape wrong and oppression.

So, in all that year, fivescore or more good stout yeomen gathered about Robin Hood, and chose him to be their leader and chief. Then they vowed that even as they themselves had been despoiled they would despoil their oppressors, whether baron, abbot, knight, or squire, and that from each they would take that which had been wrung from the poor by unjust taxes, or land rents, or in wrongful fines; but to the poor folk they would give a helping hand in need and trouble, and would return to them that which had been unjustly taken from them. Beside this, they swore never to harm a child nor to wrong a woman, be she maid, wife, or widow; so that, after a while, when the people began to find that no harm was meant to them, but that money or food came in time of want to many a poor family, they came to praise Robin and his merry men, and to tell many tales of him and of his doings in Sherwood Forest, for they felt him to be one of themselves.

Up rose Robin Hood one merry morn when all the birds were singing blithely among the leaves, and up rose all his merry men, each fellow washing his head and hands in the cold brown brook that leaped laughing from stone to stone. Then said Robin: "For fourteen days have we seen no sport, so now I will go abroad to seek adventures forthwith. But tarry ye, my merry men all, here in the greenwood; only see that ye mind well my call. Three blasts upon the bugle horn I will blow in my hour of need; then come quickly, for I shall want your aid."

So saying, he strode away through the leafy forest glades until he had come to the verge of Sherwood. There he wandered for a long time, through highway and byway, through dingly dell and forest skirts. Now he met a fair buxom lass in a shady lane, and each gave the other a merry word and passed their way; now he saw a fair lady upon an ambling pad, to whom he doffed his cap, and who bowed sedately in return to the fair youth; now he saw a fat monk on a pannier-laden ass; now a gallant knight, with spear and shield and armor that flashed brightly in the sunlight; now a page clad in crimson; and now a stout burgher from good Nottingham Town, pacing along with serious footsteps; all these sights he saw, but adventure found he none. At last he took a road by the forest skirts; a bypath that dipped toward a broad, pebbly stream spanned by a narrow bridge made of a log of wood. As he drew nigh this bridge he saw a tall stranger coming from the other side. Thereupon Robin quickened his pace, as did the stranger likewise; each thinking to cross first.

"Now stand thou back," quoth Robin, "and let the better man cross first."

"Nay," answered the stranger, "then stand back thine own self, for the better man, I wot, am I."

"That will we presently see," quoth Robin; "and meanwhile stand thou where thou art, or else, by the bright brow of Saint Ælfrida, I will show thee right good Nottingham play with a clothyard shaft betwixt thy ribs."

"Now," quoth the stranger, "I will tan thy hide till it be as many colors as a beggar's cloak, if thou darest so much as touch a string of that same bow that thou holdest in thy hands."

"Thou pratest like an ass," said Robin, "for I could send this shaft clean through thy proud heart before a curtal friar could say grace over a roast goose at Michaelmastide."

"And thou pratest like a coward," answered the stranger, "for thou standest there with a good yew bow to shoot at my heart, while I have nought in my hand but a plain blackthorn staff wherewith to meet thee."

"Now," quoth Robin, "by the faith of my heart, never have I had a coward's name in all my life before. I will lay by my trusty bow and eke my arrows, and if thou darest abide my coming, I will go and cut a cudgel to test thy manhood withal."

"Ay, marry, that will I abide thy coming, and joyously, too," quoth the stranger; whereupon he leaned sturdily upon his staff to await Robin.

Then Robin Hood stepped quickly to the coverside and cut a good staff of ground oak, straight, without flaw, and six feet in length, and came back trimming away the tender stems from it, while the stranger waited for him, leaning upon his staff, and whistling as he gazed round about. Robin observed him furtively as he trimmed his staff, measuring him from top to toe from out the corner of his eye, and thought that he had never seen a lustier or a stouter man. Tall was Robin, but taller was the stranger by a head and a neck, for he was seven feet in height. Broad was Robin across the shoulders, but broader was the stranger by twice the breadth of a palm, while he measured at least an ell around the waist.

"Nevertheless," said Robin to himself, "I will baste thy hide right merrily, my good fellow;" then, aloud, "Lo, here is my good staff, lusty and tough. Now wait my coming, an thou darest, and meet me, an thou fearest not; then we will fight until one or the other of us tumble into the stream by dint of blows."

"Marry, that meeteth my whole heart!" cried the stranger, twirling his staff above his head, betwixt his fingers and thumb, until it whistled again.

Never did the Knights of Arthur's Round Table meet in a stouter fight than did these two. In a moment Robin stepped quickly upon the bridge where the stranger stood; first he made a feint, and then delivered a blow at the stranger's head that, had it met its mark, would have tumbled him speedily into the water; but the stranger turned the blow right deftly, and in return gave one as stout, which Robin also turned as the stranger had done. So they stood, each in his place, neither moving a finger's breadth back, for one good hour, and many blows were given and received by each in that time, till here and there were sore bones and bumps, yet neither thought of crying "Enough," or seemed likely to fall from off the bridge. Now and then they stopped to rest, and each thought that he never had seen in all his life before such a hand at quarter-staff. At last Robin gave the stranger a blow upon the ribs that made his jacket smoke like a damp straw thatch in the sun. So shrewd was the stroke that the stranger came within a hair's breadth of falling off the bridge; but he regained himself right quickly, and, by a dexterous blow, gave Robin a crack on the crown that caused the blood to flow. Then Robin grew mad with anger, and smote with all his might at the other; but the stranger warded the blow, and once again thwacked Robin, and this time so fairly that he fell heels over head into the water, as the queen pin falls in a game of bowls.

"And where art thou now, good lad?" shouted the stranger, roaring with laughter.

"Oh, in the flood and floating adown with the tide," cried Robin; nor could he forbear laughing himself at his sorry plight. Then, gaining his feet, he waded to the bank, the little fish speeding hither and thither, all frightened at his splashing.

"Give me thy hand," cried he, when he had reached the bank. "I must needs own thou art a brave and a sturdy soul, and, withal, a good stout stroke with the cudgels. By this and by that, my head hummeth like to a hive of bees on a hot June day."

Then he clapped his horn to his lips, and winded a blast that went echoing sweetly down the forest paths. "Ay, marry," quoth he again, "thou art a tall lad, and eke a brave one, for ne'er, I trow, is there a man betwixt here and Canterbury Town could do the like to me that thou hast done."

"And thou," quoth the stranger, laughing, "takest thy cudgelling like a brave heart and a stout yeoman."

But now the distant twigs and branches rustled with the coming of men, and suddenly a score or two of good stout yeomen, all clad in Lincoln green, burst from out the covert, with merry Will Stutely at their head.

"Good master," cried Will, "how is this? Truly thou art all wet from head to foot, and that to the very skin."

"Why, marry," answered jolly Robin, "yon stout fellow hath tumbled me neck and crop into the water, and hath given me a drubbing beside."

"Then shall he not go without a ducking and eke a drubbing himself!" cried Will Stutely. "Have at him, lads!"

Then Will and a score of yeomen leaped upon the stranger, but though they sprang quickly they found him ready and felt him strike right and left with his stout staff, so that, though he went down with press of numbers, some of them rubbed cracked crowns before he was overcome.

"Nay, forbear!" cried Robin, laughing until his sore sides ached again; "he is a right good man and true, and no harm shall befall him. Now hark ye, good youth, wilt thou stay with me and be one of my band? Three suits of Lincoln green shalt thou have each year, beside forty marks in fee, and share with us whatsoever good shall befall us. Thou shall eat sweet venison and quaff the stoutest ale, and mine own good right-hand man shalt thou be, for never did I see such a cudgel-player in all my life before. Speak! wilt thou be one of my good merry men?"

"That I know not," quoth the stranger, surlily, for he was angry at being so tumbled about. "If ye

handle yew bow and apple shaft no better than ye
do oaken cudgel, I wot ye are not fit to be called
yeomen in my country; but if there be any man
here that can shoot a better shaft than I, then will
I bethink me of joining with you."

"Now by my faith," said Robin, "thou art a right
saucy varlet, sirrah; yet I will stoop to thee as I never
stooped to man before. Good Stutely, cut thou a fair
white piece of bark four fingers in breadth, and set
it fourscore yards distant on yonder oak. Now,
stranger, hit that fairly with a gray goose shaft and
call thyself an archer."

"Ay, marry, that will I," answered he. "Give me a
good stout bow and a fair broad arrow, and if I hit
it not strip me and beat me blue with bow-strings."

Then he chose the stoutest bow amongst them
all, next to Robin's own, and a straight gray goose
shaft, well feathered and smooth, and stepping to
the mark—while all the band, sitting or lying
upon the greensward, watched to see him shoot—
he drew the arrow to his cheek and loosed the
shaft right deftly, sending it so straight down the
path that it clove the mark in the very centre.
"Aha!" cried he, "mend thou that if thou canst;"
while even the yeomen clapped their hands at so
fair a shot.

"That is a keen shot, indeed," quoth Robin,
"mend it I cannot, but mar it I may, perhaps."

Then taking up his own good stout bow and nocking an arrow with care he shot with his very greatest skill. Straight flew the arrow, and so true that it lit fairly upon the stranger's shaft and split it into splinters. Then all the yeomen leaped to their feet and shouted for joy that their master had shot so well.

"Now by the lusty yew bow of good Saint Withold," cried the stranger, "that is a shot indeed, and never saw I the like in all my life before! Now truly will I be thy man henceforth and for aye. Good Adam Bell was a fair shot, but never shot he so!"

"Then have I gained a right good man this day," quoth jolly Robin. "What name goest thou by, good fellow."

"Men call me John Little whence I came," answered the stranger.

Then Will Stutely, who loved a good jest, spoke up. "Nay, fair little stranger," said he, "I like not thy name and fain would I have it otherwise. Little art thou indeed, and small of bone and sinew, therefore shalt thou be christened Little John, and I will be thy godfather."

Then Robin Hood and all his band laughed aloud until the stranger began to grow angry.

"An thou make a jest of me," quoth he to Will Stutely, "thou wilt have sore bones and little pay, and that in short season."

"Nay, good friend," said Robin Hood, "bottle thine anger for the name fitteth thee well. Little John shalt thou be called henceforth, and Little John shall it be. So come, my merry men, and we will go and prepare a christening feast for this fair infant."

So turning their backs upon the stream, they plunged into the forest once more, through which they traced their steps till they reached the spot where they dwelt in the depths of the woodland. There had they built huts of bark and branches of trees, and made couches of sweet rushes spread over with skins of fallow deer. Here stood a great oak tree with branches spreading broadly around, beneath which was a seat of green moss where Robin Hood was wont to sit at feast and at merrymaking with his stout men about him. Here they found the rest of the band, some of whom had come in with a brace of fat does. Then they all built great fires and after a time roasted the does and broached a barrel of humming ale. Then when the feast was ready they all sat down, but Robin Hood placed Little John at his right hand, for he was henceforth to be the second in the band.

Then when the feast was done Will Stutely spoke up. "It is now time, I ween, to christen our bonny babe, is it not so, merry boys?" And "Aye! Aye!" cried all, laughing till the woods echoed with their mirth.

"Then seven sponsors shall we have," quoth Will Stutely; and hunting among all the band he chose the seven stoutest men of them all.

"Now by Saint Dunstan," cried Little John, springing to his feet, "more than one of you shall rue it an you lay finger on me."

But without a word they all ran upon him at once, seizing him by his legs and arms and holding him tightly in spite of his struggles, and they bore him forth while all stood around to see the sport, Then one came forward who had been chosen to play the priest because he had a bald crown, and in his hand he carried a brimming pot of ale. "Now who bringeth this babe?" asked he right soberly.

"That do I," answered Will Stutely.

"And what name callest thou him?"

"Little John call I him."

"Now Little John," quoth the mock priest, "thou hast not lived heretofore, but only got thee along through the world, but henceforth thou wilt live indeed. When thou livedst not thou wast called John Little, but now that thou dost live indeed, Little John shalt thou be called, so christen I thee." And at these last words he emptied the pot of ale upon Little John's head.

Then all shouted with laughter as they saw the good brown ale stream over Little John's beard and trickle from his nose and chin, while his eyes blinked with the smart of it. At first he was of a mind to be angry, but found he could not because the others were so merry; so he, too, laughed with the rest. Then Robin took this sweet, pretty babe, clothed him all anew from top to toe in Lincoln green, and gave him a good stout bow, and so made him a member of the merry band.

And thus it was that Robin Hood became outlawed; thus a band of merry companions gathered about him, and thus he gained his right-hand man, Little John.

THE SHOOTING-MATCH AT NOTTINGHAM TOWN

Then the Sheriff was very wroth because of this failure to take jolly Robin, for it came to his ears, as ill news always does, that the people laughed at him and made a jest of this thinking to serve a warrant upon such a one as the bold outlaw; and a man hates nothing so much as being made a jest of; so he said: "Our gracious Lord and Sovereign King himself shall know of this, and how his laws are perverted and despised by this band of rebel outlaws. As for yon traitor Tinker, him will I hang, if I catch him, upon the very highest gallows tree in all Nottinghamshire."

Then he bade all his servants and retainers to make ready to go to London town, to see and speak with the King.

At this there was bustling at the Sheriff's castle, and men ran hither and thither upon this business and upon that, while the forge fires of Nottingham glowed red far into the night like twinkling stars, for all the smiths of the town were busy making or mending armor for the Sheriff's troop of escort. For two days this labor lasted, then, on the third, all was ready for the journey. So forth they started in the bright sunlight, from Nottingham Town to Fosse Way and thence to Watling Street; and so they journeyed for two days, until they saw at last the spires and towers of great London Town; and many folks stopped, as they journeyed along, and gazed at the show they made riding along the highways with their flashing armor, and gay plumes and trappings.

In London King Henry and his fair Queen Elinor held their court, gay with ladies in silks and satins and velvets and cloth of gold, and also brave knights and gallant courtiers. Thither came the Sheriff and was shown into the King's presence.

"A boon, a boon," quoth he, as he knelt upon the ground.

"Now what wouldst thou have?" said the King. "Let us hear what may be thy desires."

"O good my Lord and Sovereign," spake the Sheriff, "in Sherwood Forest, in our own good shire of Nottingham, liveth a bold outlaw whose name is Robin Hood."

"In good sooth," said the King, "his doings have reached even our own royal ears. He is a saucy, rebellious varlet, yet, I am fain to own, a right merry soul withal."

"But hearken, O my most gracious Sovereign," said the Sheriff. "I sent a warrant to him with thine own royal seal attached, by a right lusty knave, but he beat the messenger and stole the warrant. And he killeth thy deer and robbeth thine own liege subjects even upon the great highways."

"Why, how now," quoth the King, wrathfully. "What wouldst thou have me do? Comest thou not to me with a great array of men-at-arms and retainers, and yet art not able to take a single band of lusty knaves without armor on breast, in thine own county! What wouldst thou have me do? Art thou not my Sheriff? Are not my laws in force in Nottinghamshire? Canst thou not take thine own course against those that break the laws or do an injury to thee or thine? Go, get thee gone, and think well; devise some plan of thine own but trouble me no further. But look well to it, master Sheriff, for I will have my laws obeyed by all men within my kingdom, and if thou art not able to enforce them thou art no sheriff for me. So look well to thyself, I say, or ill may befall thee as well as all the thieving knaves in Nottinghamshire. When the flood cometh it sweepeth away grain as well as chaff."

Then the Sheriff turned away with a sore and troubled heart, and sadly he rued his fine show of retainers, for he saw that the King was angry because he had so many men about him and yet could not enforce the laws. So, as they all rode slowly back to Nottingham, the Sheriff was thoughtful and full of care. Not a word did he speak to any one, and no one of his men spoke to him, but all the time he was busy devising some plan to take Robin Hood.

"Aha!" cried he suddenly, smiting his hand upon his thigh, "I have it now! Ride on, my merry men all, and let us get back to Nottingham Town as speedily as we may. And mark well my words: before a fortnight is passed, that evil knave, Robin Hood, will be safely clapped into Nottingham gaol."

But what was the Sheriff's plan?

As a Jew takes each one of a bag of silver angels, feeling each coin to find whether it be clipped or not, so the Sheriff, as all rode slowly and sadly back toward Nottingham, took up thought after thought in turn, feeling around the edges of each but finding in every one some flaw. At last he thought of the daring soul of jolly Robin and how, as he the Sheriff knew, he often came even within the walls of Nottingham.

"Now," thought the Sheriff, "could I but persuade Robin nigh to Nottingham Town so that I could find him, I warrant I would lay hands upon him so stoutly that he would never get away again." Then of a sudden it came to him like a flash that were he to proclaim a great shooting-match and offer some grand prize, Robin Hood might be over-persuaded by his spirit to come to the butts; and it was this thought which caused him to cry, "Aha!" and smite his palm upon his thigh.

So, as soon as he had returned safely to Nottingham, he sent messengers north and south, and east and west, to proclaim through town, hamlet, and countryside, this grand shooting-match, and every one was bidden that could draw a long bow, and the prize was to be an arrow of pure beaten gold.

When Robin Hood first heard the news of this he was in Lincoln Town, and hastening back to Sherwood Forest he soon called all his merry men about him and spoke to them thus:—

"Now hearken, my merry men all, to the news that I have brought from Lincoln Town to-day. Our friend the Sheriff of Nottingham hath proclaimed a shooting-match, and hath sent messengers to tell of it through all the country side, and the prize is to be a bright golden arrow. Now I fain would have one of us win it, both because of the fairness of the prize and because our sweet friend the Sheriff hath offered it. So we will take our bows and shafts and go there to shoot, for I know right well that merriment will be a-going. What say ye, lads?"

Then young David of Doncaster spoke up and said: "Now listen, I pray thee, good master, unto what I say. I have come straight from our friend Eadom o' the Blue Boar, and there I heard the full news of this same match. But, master, I know from him, and he got it from the Sheriff's man Ralph o' the Scar, that this same knavish Sheriff hath but laid a trap for thee in this shooting-match and wishes nothing so much as to see thee there. So go not, good master, for I know right well he doth seek to beguile thee, but stay within the greenwood lest we all meet dole and woe."

"Now," quoth Robin, "thou art a wise lad and keepest thine ears open and thy mouth shut, as becometh a wise and crafty woodsman. But shall we let it be said that the Sheriff of Nottingham did cow bold Robin Hood and seven-score as fair archers as are in all merry England? Nay, good David, what thou tellest me maketh me to desire the prize even more than I else should do. But what sayeth our good gossip Swanthold? is it not 'A hasty man burneth his mouth, and the fool that keepeth his eyes

shut falleth into the pit?' Thus he says, truly, therefore we must meet guile with guile. Now some of
you clothe yourselves as curtal friars, and some as
rustic peasants, and some as tinkers, or as beggars,
but see that each man taketh a good bow or
broadsword, in case need should arise. As for myself,
I will shoot for this same golden arrow, and should
I win it, we will hang it to the branches of our good
greenwood tree for the joy of all the band. How like
you the plan, my merry men all?"

Then, "good, good!" cried all the band right
heartily.

A fair sight was Nottingham Town on the day of
the shooting-match. All along upon the green
meadow beneath the town wall stretched a row of
benches, one above the other, which were for
knight and lady, squire and dame, and rich burghers
and their wives; for none but those of rank and
quality were to sit there. At the end of the range,
near the target, was a raised seat bedecked with rib-
bons and scarfs and garlands of flowers, for the Sheriff of Nottingham and his dame. The range was two
score paces broad. At one end stood the target, at the
other a tent of striped canvas, from the pole of
which fluttered many-colored flags and streamers.
In this booth were casks of ale, free to be broached
by any of the archers who might wish to quench
their thirst.

Across the range from where the seats for the better folk were raised was a railing to keep the poorer people from crowding in front of the target. Already, while it was early, the benches were beginning to fill with people of quality, who kept constantly arriving in little carts, or upon palfreys that curveted gayly to the merry tinkle of silver bells at bridle-reins; with these came also the poorer folk, who sat or lay upon the green grass near the railing that kept them from off the range. In the great tent the archers were gathering by twos and threes; some talking loudly of the fair shots each man had made in his day; some looking well to their bows, drawing a sting betwixt the fingers to see that there was no fray upon it, or inspecting arrows, shutting one eye and peering down a shaft to see that it was not warped, but straight and true, for neither bow nor shaft should fail at such a time and for such a prize. And never were such a company of yeomen as were gathered at Nottingham Town that day, for the very best archers of merry England had come to this shooting-match. There was Gill o' the Red Cap, the Sheriff's own head archer, and Diccon Cruikshank of Lincoln Town, and Adam o' the Dell, a man of Tamworth, of threescore years and more, yet hale and lusty still, who in his time had shot in the famous match at Woodstock, and had there beaten that renowned archer, Clym o' the Clough. And many more famous men of the long bow were there, whose names have been handed down to us in goodly ballads of the olden time.

But now all the benches were filled with guests, lord and lady, burgher and dame, when at last the Sheriff himself came with his lady, he riding with stately mien upon his milk-white horse and she upon her brown filly. Upon his head he wore a purple velvet cap, and purple velvet was his robe, all trimmed about with rich ermine; his jerkin and hose were of sea-green silk, and his shoes of black velvet, the pointed toes fastened to his garters with golden chains. A golden chain hung about his neck, and at his collar was a great carbuncle set in red gold. His lady was dressed in blue velvet, all trimmed with swan's down. So they made a gallant sight as they rode along side by side, and all the people shouted from where they crowded across the space from the gentle-folk; so the Sheriff and his lady came to their place, where men-at-arms, with hauberk and spear, stood about, waiting for them.

Then when the Sheriff and his dame had sat down, he bade his herald wind upon his silver horn; who thereupon sounded three blasts that came echoing cheerily back from the gray walls of Nottingham. Then the archers stepped forth to their places, while all the folk shouted with a mighty voice, each man calling upon his favorite yeoman. "Red Cap!" cried some; "Cruikshank!" cried others; "Hey for William O'Leslie!" shouted others yet again; while ladies waved silken scarfs to urge each yeoman to do his best.

Then the herald stood forth and loudly proclaimed the rules of the game as follows:—

"Shoot each man from yon mark, which is seven-score yards and ten from the target. One arrow shooteth each man first, and from all the archers shall the ten that shooteth the fairest shafts be chosen for to shoot again. Two arrows shooteth each man of these ten, then shall the three that shoot the fairest shafts be chosen for to shoot again. Three arrows shooteth each man of those three, and to him that shooteth the fairest shafts shall the prize be given."

Then the Sheriff leaned forward, looking keenly among the press of archers to find whether Robin Hood was amongst them; but no one was there clad in Lincoln green, such as was worn by Robin and his band. "Nevertheless," said the Sheriff to himself, "he may still be there, and I miss him among the crowd of other men. But let me see when but ten men shoot, for I wot he will be among the ten, or I know him not."

And now the archers shot, each man in turn, and the good folk never saw such archery as was done that day. Six arrows were within the clout, four

within the black, and only two smote the outer
ring; so that when the last arrow sped and struck
the target, all the people shouted aloud, for it was
noble shooting.

And now but ten men were left of all those that
had shot before, and of these ten, six were famous
throughout the land, and most of the folk gathered
there knew them. These six men were Gilbert o' the
Red Cap, Adam o' the Dell, Diccon Cruikshank,
William o' Leslie, Hubert o' Cloud, and Swithin o'
Hertford. Two others were yeomen of merry York-
shire, another was a tall stranger in blue, who said he
came from London Town, and the last was a tattered
stranger in scarlet, who wore a patch over one eye.

"Now," quoth the Sheriff to a man-at-arms who
stood near him, "seest thou Robin Hood among
those ten?"

"Nay, that I do not, your worship," answered the
man. "Six of them I know right well. Of those York-
shire yeomen, one is too tall and the other too short
for that bold knave. Robin's beard is as yellow as
gold, while yon tattered beggar in scarlet hath a
beard of brown, besides being blind of one eye. As
for the stranger in blue, Robin's shoulders, I ween,
are three inches broader than his."

"Then," quoth the Sheriff, smiting his thigh an-
grily, "yon knave is a coward as well as a rogue, and
dares not show his face among good men and true."

Then, after they had rested a short time, those ten stout men stepped forth to shoot again. Each man shot two arrows, and as they shot, not a word was spoken, but all the crowd watched with scarce a breath of sound; but when the last had shot his arrow another great shout arose, while many cast their caps aloft for joy of such marvellous shooting.

"Now by our gracious Lady fair," quoth old Sir Amyas o' the Dell, who, bowed with fourscore years and more, sat near the Sheriff, "ne'er saw I such archery in all my life before, yet have I seen the best hands at the long bow for threescore years and more."

And now but three men were left of all those that had shot before. One was Gill o' the Red Cap, one the tattered stranger in scarlet, and one Adam o' the Dell of Tamworth Town. Then all the people called aloud, some crying, "Ho for Gilbert o' the Red Cap!" and some, "Hey for stout Adam o' Tamworth!" but not a single man in the crowd called upon the stranger in scarlet.

"Now, shoot thou well, Gilbert," cried the Sheriff, "and if thine be the best shaft, fivescore broad silver pennies will I give to thee beside the prize."

"Truly I will do my best," quoth Gilbert, right sturdily. "A man cannot do aught but his best, but that will I strive to do this day." So saying, he drew forth a fair smooth arrow with a broad feather and fitted it deftly to the string, then drawing his bow with care he sped the shaft. Straight flew the arrow and lit fairly in the clout, a finger breadth from the centre. "A Gilbert, a Gilbert!" shouted all the crowd; and, "Now, by my faith," cried the Sheriff, smiting his hands together, "that is a shrewd shot."

Then the tattered stranger stepped forth, and all the people laughed as they saw a yellow patch that showed beneath his arm when he raised his elbow to shoot, and also to see him aim with but one eye. He drew the good yew bow quickly, and quickly loosed a shaft; so short was the time that no man could draw a breath betwixt the drawing and the shooting; yet his arrow lodged nearer the centre than the other by twice the length of a barleycorn.

"Now by all the saints in Paradise!" cried the Sheriff, "that is a lovely shaft in very truth!"

Then Adam o' the Dell shot, carefully and cautiously, and his arrow lodged close beside the stranger's. Then after a short space they all three shot again, and once more each arrow lodged within the clout, but this time Adam o' the Dell's was farthest from the centre, and again the tattered stranger's shot was the best. Then, after another time of rest, they all shot for the third time. This time Gilbert took great heed to his aim, keenly measuring the distance and shooting with shrewdest care. Straight flew the arrow, and all shouted till the very flags that waved in the breeze shook with the sound, and the rooks and daws flew clamoring about the roofs of the old gray tower, for the shaft had lodged close beside the spot that marked the very centre.

"Well done, Gilbert!" cried the Sheriff, right joyously. "Fain am I to believe the prize is thine, and right fairly won. Now, thou ragged knave, let me see thee shoot a better shaft than that."

Naught spake the stranger but took his place, while all was hushed, and no one spoke or even seemed to breathe, so great was the silence for wonder what he would do. Meanwhile, also, quite still stood the stranger holding his bow in his hand, while one could count five; then he drew his trusty yew, holding it drawn but a moment, then loosed the string. Straight flew the arrow, and so true that it smote a gray goose feather from off Gilbert's shaft, which fell fluttering through the sunlit air as the stranger's arrow lodged close beside his of the red cap, and in the very centre. No one spoke a word for a while and no one shouted, but each man looked into his neighbor's face amazedly.

"Nay," quoth old Adam o' the Dell presently, drawing a long breath and shaking his head as he spoke; "twoscore years and more have I shot shaft, and maybe not all times bead, but I shoot no more this day, for no man can match with yon stranger, whosoe'er he may be." Then he thrust his shaft into his quiver, rattling, and unstrung his bow without another word.

Then the Sheriff came down from his dais and drew near, in all his silks and velvets, to where the tattered stranger stood leaning upon his stout bow, whilst the good folk crowded around to see the man who shot so wondrously well. "Here, good fellow," quoth the Sheriff, "take thou the prize, and well and fairly hast thou won it, I trow. What may be thy name, and whence comest thou?"

"Men do call me Jock o' Teviotdale, and thence am I come," said the stranger.

"Then, by Our Lady, Jock, thou art the fairest archer that e'er mine eyes beheld, and if thou wilt join my service I will clothe thee with a better coat than that thou has upon thy back; thou shalt eat and drink of the best, and at every Christmas-tide fourscore marks shall by thy wage. I trow thou drawest better bow than that same coward knave, Robin Hood, that dared not show his face here this day. Say, good fellow, wilt thou join my service?"

"Nay, that will I not," quoth the stranger, roughly. "I will be mine own, and no man in all merry England shall be my master."

"Then get thee gone, and a murrain seize thee!" cried the Sheriff, and his voice trembled with anger. "And by my faith and troth I have a good part of a mind to have thee beaten for thine insolence!" Then he turned upon his heel and strode away.

It was a right motley company that gathered about the noble greenwood tree in Sherwood's depths that same day. A score and more of barefoot friars were there, and some that looked like tinkers, and some that seemed to be sturdy beggars and rustic hinds; and seated upon a mossy couch was one all clad in tattered scarlet, with a patch over one eye; and in his hand he held the golden arrow that was the prize of the great shooting-match. Then, amidst a noise of talking and laughter, he took the patch from off his eye and stripped away the scarlet rags from off his body and showed himself all clothed in fair Lincoln green, and quoth he: "Easy come these things away, but walnut stain cometh not so speedily from yellow hair." Then all laughed louder than before, for it was Robin Hood himself that had won the prize from the Sheriff's very hands.

Then all sat down to the woodland feast and talked amongst themselves of the merry jest that had been played upon the Sheriff, and of the adventures that had befallen each member of the band in his disguise. But when the feast was done, Robin Hood took Little John apart and said, "Truly am I vexed in my blood, for I heard the Sheriff say today, 'Thou shootest better than that coward knave, Robin Hood, that dared not show his face here this day.' I would fain let him know who it was who won the golden arrow from out his hand, and also that I am no coward such as he takes me to be."

Then Little John said, "Good master, take thou me and Will Stutely and we will send yon fat Sheriff news of all this by a messenger such as he doth not expect."

That day the Sheriff sat at meat in the great hall of his house at Nottingham Town. Long tables stood down the hall, at which sat men-at-arms and household servants and good stout villains, in all fourscore and more. There they talked of the day's shooting as they ate their meat and quaffed their ale. The Sheriff sat at the head of the table upon a raised seat under a canopy, and beside him sat his dame.

"By my troth," said he, "I did reckon full roundly that that knave, Robin Hood, would be at the game to-day. I did not think that he was such a coward. But who could that saucy knave be who answered me to my beard so bravely? I wonder that I did not have him beaten; but there was something about him that spoke of other things than rags and tatters."

Then, even as he finished speaking, something fell rattling among the dishes on the table, while those that sat near started up wondering what it might be. After a while one of the men-at-arms gathered courage enough to pick it up and bring it to the Sheriff. Then every one saw that it was a blunted gray goose shaft, with a fine scroll, about the thickness of a goose quill, tied near to its head. The Sheriff opened the scroll and glanced at it, while the veins upon his forehead swelled and his cheeks grew ruddy with rage as he read, for this was what he saw:—

"Now Heaven bless thy grace this day,
Say all in sweet Sherwood,
For thou didst give the prize away
To merry Robin Hood."

"Whence came this?" cried the Sheriff in a mighty voice.

"Even through the window, your worship," quoth the man who had handed the shaft to him.

Tarzan

[EDGAR RICE BURROUGHS]

TARZAN RESCUES THE MOON

The moon shone down out of a cloudless sky—a huge, swollen moon that seemed so close to earth that one might wonder that she did not brush the crooning tree tops. It was night, and Tarzan was abroad in the jungle—Tarzan, the ape-man; mighty fighter, mighty hunter. Why he swung through the dark shadows of the somber forest he could not have told you. It was not that he was hungry—he had fed well this day, and in a safe cache were the remains of his kill, ready against the coming of a new appetite. Perhaps it was the very joy of living that urged him from his arboreal couch to pit his muscles and his senses against the jungle night, and then, too, Tarzan always was goaded by an intense desire to know.

The jungle which is presided over by Kudu, the sun, is a very different jungle from that of Goro, the moon. The diurnal jungle has its own aspect—its own lights and shades, its own birds, its own blooms, its own beasts; its noises are the noises of the day. The lights and shades of the nocturnal jungle are as different as one might imagine the lights and shades of another world to differ from those of our world; its beasts, its blooms, and its birds are not those of the jungle of Kudu, the sun.

Because of these differences Tarzan loved to investigate the jungle by night. Not only was the life another life; but it was richer in numbers and in romance; it was richer in dangers, too, and to Tarzan of the Apes danger was the spice of life. And the noises of the jungle night—the roar of the lion, the scream of the leopard, the hideous laughter of the Dango, the hyena, were music to the ears of the ape-man.

The soft padding of unseen feet, the rustling of leaves and grasses to the passage of fierce beasts, the sheen of opalesque eyes flaming through the dark, the million sounds which proclaimed the teeming life that one might hear and scent, though seldom see, constituted the appeal of the nocturnal jungle to Tarzan.

Tonight he had swung a wide circle—toward the east first and then toward the south, and now he was rounding back again into the north. His eyes, his ears and his keen nostrils were ever on the alert. Mingled

with the sounds he knew, there were strange sounds—
weird sounds which he never heard until after Kudu
had sought his lair below the far edge of the big
water—sounds which belonged to Goro, the moon—
and to the mysterious period of Goro's supremacy.
The sounds often caused Tarzan profound specula-
tion. They baffled him because he thought that he
knew his jungle so well that there could be nothing
within it unfamiliar to him. Sometimes he thought
that as colors and forms appeared to differ by night
from their familiar daylight aspects, so sounds altered
with the passage of Kudu and the coming of Goro,
and these thoughts roused within his brain a vague
conjecture that perhaps Goro and Kudu influenced
these changes. And what more natural that eventually
he came to attribute to the sun and the moon per-
sonalities as real as his own? The sun was a living creature and ruled the day. The moon, endowed with
brains and miraculous powers, ruled the night.

Thus functioned the untrained man-mind grop-
ing through the dark night of ignorance for an explanation of the things he could not touch or smell
or hear and of the great, unknown powers of nature
which he could not see.

As Tarzan swung north again upon his wide circle
the scent of the Gomangani came to his nostrils,
mixed with the acrid odor of wood smoke. The ape-
man moved quickly in the direction from which the

scent was borne down to him upon the gentle night wind. Presently the ruddy sheen of a great fire filtered through the foliage to him ahead, and when Tarzan came to a halt in the trees near it, he saw a party of half a dozen black warriors huddled close to the blaze. It was evidently a hunting party from the village of Mbonga, the chief, caught out in the jungle after dark. In a rude circle about them they had constructed a thorn boma which, with the aid of the fire, they apparently hoped would discourage the advances of the larger carnivora.

That hope was not conviction was evidenced by the very palpable terror in which they crouched, wide-eyed and trembling, for already Numa and Sabor were moaning through the jungle toward them. There were other creatures, too, in the shadows beyond the firelight. Tarzan could see their yellow eyes flaming there. The blacks saw them and shivered. Then one arose and grasping a burning branch from the fire hurled it at the eyes, which immediately disappeared. The black sat down again. Tarzan watched and saw that it was several minutes before the eyes began to reappear in twos and fours.

Then came Numa, the lion, and Sabor, his mate. The other eyes scattered to the right and left before the menacing growls of the great cats, and then the huge orbs of the man-eaters flamed alone out of the darkness. Some of the blacks threw themselves upon their faces and moaned; but he who before had hurled the burning branch now hurled another straight at the faces of the hungry lions, and they, too, disappeared as had the lesser lights before them. Tarzan was much interested. He saw a new reason for the nightly fires maintained by the blacks—a reason in addition those connected with warmth and light and cooking. The beasts of the jungle feared fire, and so fire was, in a measure, a protection from them. Tarzan himself knew a certain awe of fire. Once he had, in investigating an abandoned fire in the village of the blacks, picked up a live coal. Since then he had maintained a respectful distance from such fires as he had seen. On experience had sufficed.

For a few minutes after the black hurled the fire-brand no eyes appeared, though Tarzan could hear the soft padding of feet all about him. Then flashed once more the twin fire spots that marked the re-turn of the lord of the jungle and a moment later, upon a slightly lower level, there appeared those of Sabor, his mate.

For some time they remained fixed and unwaver-ing—a constellation of fierce stars in the jungle night—then the male lion advanced slowly toward the boma, where all but a single black still crouched in trembling terror. When this lone guardian saw that Numa was again approaching, he threw another firebrand, and, as before, Numa retreated and with him Sabor, the lioness; but not so far, this time, nor for so long. Almost instantly they turned and began circling the boma, their eyes turning constantly toward the firelight, while low, throaty growls evidenced their increasing displeasure. Beyond the lions glowed the flaming eyes of the lesser satellites, until the black jungle was shot all around the black men's camp with little spots of fire.

Again and again the black warrior hurled his puny brands at the two big cats; but Tarzan noticed that Numa paid little or no attention to them after the first few retreats. The ape-man knew by Numa's voice that the lion was hungry and surmised that he had made up his mind to feed upon a Gomangani; but would he dare a closer approach to the dreaded flames?

Even as the thought was passing in Tarzan's mind, Numa stopped his restless pacing and faced the boma. For a moment he stood motionless, except for the quick, nervous upcurving of his tail, then he walked deliberately forward, while Sabor moved restlessly to and fro where he had left her. The black man called to his comrades that the lion was coming, but they were too far gone in fear to do more than huddle closer together and moan more loudly than before.

Seizing a blazing branch the man cast it straight into the face of the lion. There was an angry roar, followed by a swift charge. With a single bound the savage beast cleared the boma wall as, with almost

equal agility, the warrior cleared it upon the opposite side and, chancing the dangers lurking in the
darkness, bolted for the nearest tree.

Numa was out of the boma almost as soon as he
was inside it; but as he went back over the low thorn
wall, he took a screaming negro with him. Dragging
his victim along the ground he walked back toward
Sabor, the lioness, who joined him, and the two
continued into the blackness, their savage growls
mingling with the piercing shrieks of the doomed
and terrified man.

At a little distance from the blaze the lions halted,
there ensued a short succession of unusually vicious
growls and roars, during which the cries and moans
of the black man ceased—forever.

Presently Numa reappeared in the firelight. He
made a second trip into the boma and the former
grisly tragedy was reënacted with another howling victim.

Tarzan rose and stretched lazily. The entertainment was beginning to bore him. He yawned and
turned upon his way toward the clearing where the
tribe would be sleeping in the encircling trees.

Yet even when he had found his familiar crotch
and curled himself for slumber, he felt no desire to
sleep. For a long time he lay awake thinking and
dreaming. He looked up into the heavens and
watched the moon and the stars. He wondered what

they were and what power kept them from falling. He was an inquisitive mind. Always he had been full of questions concerning all that passed around him; but there never had been one to answer his questions. In childhood he had wanted to *know,* and, denied almost all knowledge, he still, in manhood, was filled with the great, unsatisfied curiosity of a child.

He was never quite content merely to perceive that things happened—he desired to know *why* they happened. He wanted to know what made things go. The secret of life interested him immensely. The miracle of death he could not quite fathom. Upon innumerable occasions he had investigated the internal mechanism of his kills, and once or twice he had opened the chest cavity of victims in time to see the heart still pumping.

He had learned from experience that a knife thrust through this organ brought immediate death nine times out of ten, while he might stab an antagonist innumerable times in other places without even disabling him. And so he had come to think of the heart, or, as he called it, "the red thing that breathes," as the seat and origin of life.

The brain and its functionings he did not comprehend at all. That his sense perceptions were transmitted to his brain and there translated, classified, and labeled was something quite beyond him. He thought that his fingers knew when they touched something, that his eyes knew when they saw, his ears when they heard, his nose when it scented.

He considered his throat, epidermis, and the hairs of his head as the three pincipal seats of emotion. When Kala had been slain a peculiar choking sensation had possessed his throat; contact with Histah, the snake, imparted an unpleasant sensation to the skin of his whole body; while the approach of an enemy made the hairs on his scalp stand erect.

Imagine, if you can, a child filled with the wonders of nature, bursting with queries and surrounded only by beasts of the jungle to whom his questionings were as strange as Sanskrit would have been. If he asked Gunto what made it rain, the big old ape would but gaze at him in dumb astonishment for an instant and then return to his interesting and edifying search for fleas; and when he questioned Mumga, who was very old and should have been very wise, but wasn't, as to the reason for the closing of certain flowers after Kudu had deserted the sky, and the opening of others during the night, he was surprised to discover that Mumga had never noticed these interesting facts, though she could tell to an inch just where the fattest grubworm should be hiding.

To Tarzan these things were wonders. They appealed to his intellect and to his imagination. He saw the flowers close and open; he saw certain blooms which turned their faces always toward the sun; he saw leaves which moved when there was no breeze; he saw vines crawl like living things up the boles and over the branches of great trees; and to Tarzan of the Apes the flowers and the vines and the trees were living creatures. He often talked to them, as he talked to Goro, the moon, and Kudu, the sun, and always was he disappointed that they did not reply. He asked them questions; but they could not answer, though he knew that the whispering of the leaves was the language of the leaves—they talked with one another.

The wind he attributed to the trees and the grasses. He thought that they swayed themselves to and fro, creating the wind. In no other way could he account for this phenomenon. The rain he finally attributed to the stars, the moon, and the sun; but his hypothesis was entirely unlovely and unpoetical.

Tonight as Tarzan lay thinking, there sprang to his fertile imagination an explanation of the stars and the moon. He became quite excited about it. Taug was sleeping in a near-by crotch. Tarzan swung over beside him.

"Taug!" he cried. Instantly the great bull was awake and bristling, sensing danger from the nocturnal summons. "Look, Taug!" exclaimed Tarzan, pointing toward the stars. "See the eyes of Numa and Sabor, of Sheeta and Dango. They wait around Goro to leap in upon him for their kill. See the eyes and the nose and the mouth of Goro. And the light that shines upon his face is the light of the great fire he has built to frighten away Numa and Sabor and Dango and Sheeta.

"All about him are the eyes, Taug, you can see them! But they do not come very close to the fire—there are few eyes close to Goro. They fear the fire! It is the fire that saves Goro from Numa. Do you see them, Taug? Some night Numa will be very hungry and very angry—then he will leap over the thorn bushes which encircle Goro and we will have no more light after Kudu seeks his lair—the night will be black with the blackness that comes when Goro is lazy and sleeps late into the night, or when he wanders through the skies by day, forgetting the jungle and its people."

Taug looked stupidly at the heavens and then at Tarzan. A meteor fell, blazing a flaming way through the sky.

"Look!" cried Tarzan. "Goro has thrown a burning branch at Numa."

Taug grumbled. "Numa is down below," he said. "Numa does not hunt above the trees." But he looked curiously and a little fearfully at the bright stars above him, as though he saw them for the first time, and doubtless it was the first time that Taug ever had seen the stars, though they had been in the sky above him every night of his life. To Taug they were as the gorgeous jungle blooms—he could not eat them and so he ignored them.

Taug fidgeted and was nervous. For a long time he lay sleepless, watching the stars—the flaming eyes of the beasts of prey surrounding Goro, the moon—Goro, by whose light the apes danced to the beating of their earthen drums. If Goro should be eaten by Numa there could be no more Dum-Dums. Taug was overwhelmed by the thought. He glanced at Tarzan half fearfully. Why was his friend so different from the others of the tribe? No one else whom Taug ever had known had had such queer thoughts as Tarzan. The ape scratched his head and wondered, dimly, if Tarzan was a safe companion, and then he recalled slowly, and by a laborious mental process, that Tarzan had served him better than any other of the apes, even the strong and wise bulls of the tribe.

Tarzan it was who had freed him from the blacks at the very time that Taug had thought Tarzan wanted Teeka. It was Tarzan who had saved Taug's little balu from death. It was Tarzan who had conceived and carried out the plan to pursue Teeka's abductor and rescue the stolen one. Tarzan had fought and bled in Taug's service so many times that Taug, although only a brutal ape, had had impressed upon his mind a fierce loyalty which nothing now could swerve—his friendship for Tarzan had become a habit, a tradition almost, which would endure while Taug endured. He never showed any outward demonstration of affection—he growled at Tarzan as he growled at the other bulls who came too close while he was feeding—but he would have died for Tarzan. He knew it and Tarzan knew it; but of such things apes do not speak—their vocabulary, for the finer instincts, consisting more of actions than words. But now Taug was worried, and he fell asleep again still thinking of the strange words of his fellow.

The following day he thought of them again, and without any intention of disloyalty he mentioned to Gunto what Tarzan had suggested about the eyes surrounding Goro, and the possibility that sooner or later Numa would charge the moon and devour him. To the apes all large things in nature are male, and so Goro, being the largest creature in the heavens by night, was, to them, a bull.

Gunto bit a sliver from a horny finger and recalled the fact that Tarzan had once said that the trees talked to one another, and Gozan recounted having seen the ape-man dancing alone in the moonlight with Sheeta, the panther. They did not know that Tarzan had roped the savage beast and tied him to a tree before he came to earth and leaped about before the rearing cat, to tantalize him.

Others told of seeing Tarzan ride upon the back of Tantor, the elephant; of his bringing the black boy, Tibo, to the tribe, and of mysterious things with which he communed in the strange lair by the sea.

They had never understood his books, and after he had shown them to one or two of the tribe and discovered that even the pictures carried no impression to their brains, he had desisted.

"Tarzan is not an ape," said Gunto. "He will bring Numa to eat us, as he is bringing him to eat Goro. We should kill him."

Immediately Taug bristled. Kill Tarzan! "First you will kill Taug," he said, and lumbered away to search for food.

But others joined the plotters. They thought of many things which Tarzan had done—things which apes did not do and could not understand. Again Gunto voiced the opinion that the Tarmangani, the white ape, should be slain, and the others, filled with terror about the stories they had heard, and thinking Tarzan was planning to slay Goro, greeted the proposal with growls of accord.

Among them was Teeka, listening with all her ears; but her voice was not raised in furtherance of the plan. Instead she bristled, showing her fangs, and afterward she went away in search of Tarzan; but she could not find him, as he was roaming far afield in search of meat. She found Taug, though, and told him what the others were planning, and the great bull stamped upon the ground and roared. His blood-shot eyes blazed with wrath, his upper lip curled up to expose his fighting fangs, and the hair upon his spine stood erect, and then a rodent scurried across the open and Taug sprang to seize it. In an instant he seemed to have forgotten his rage against the enemies of his friend; but such is the mind of an ape.

Several miles away Tarzan of the Apes lolled upon the broad head of Tantor, the elephant. He scratched beneath the great ears with the point of a sharp stick, and he talked to the huge pachyderm of everything which filled his black-thatched head. Little, or nothing, of what he said did Tantor understand; but Tantor is a good listener. Swaying from side to side he stood there enjoying the companionship of his friend, the friend he loved, and absorbing the delicious sensations of the scratching.

Numa, the lion, caught the scent of man, and warily stalked it until he came within sight of his prey upon the head of the mighty tusker; then he turned, growling and muttering, away in search of more propitious hunting grounds.

The elephant caught the scent of the lion, borne to him by an eddying breeze, and lifting his trunk trumpeted loudly. Tarzan stretched back luxuriously, lying supine at full length along the rough hide. Flies swarmed about his face; but with a leafy branch torn from a tree he lazily brushed them away.

"Tantor," he said, "it is good to be alive. It is good to lie in the cool shadows. It is good to look upon the green trees and the bright colors of the flowers—upon everything which Bulamutumumo has put here for us. He is very good to us, Tantor; He has given you tender leaves and bark, and rich grasses to eat; to me He has given Bara and Horta and Pisah, the fruits and the nuts and the roots. He provides for each the food that each likes best. All that He asks is that we be strong enough or cunning enough to go forth and take it. Yes, Tantor, it is good to live. I should hate to die."

Tantor made a little sound in his throat and curled his trunk upward that he might caress the ape-man's cheek with the finger at its tip.

"Tantor," said Tarzan presently, "turn and feed in the direction of the tribe of Kerchak, the great ape, that Tarzan may ride home upon your head without walking."

The tusker turned and moved slowly off along a broad, tree-arched trail, pausing occasionally to pluck a tender branch, or strip the edible bark from an adjacent tree. Tarzan sprawled face downward upon the beast's head and back, his legs hanging on either side, his head supported by his open palms, his elbows resting on the broad cranium. And thus they made their leisurely way toward the gathering place of the tribe.

Just before they arrived at the clearing from the north there reached it from the south another fig-ure—that of a well-knit black warrior, who stepped cautiously through the jungle, every sense upon the alert against the many dangers which might lurk anywhere along the way. Yet he passed beneath the southernmost sentry that was posted in a great tree commanding the trail from the south. The ape permitted the Gomangani to pass unmolested, for he saw that he was alone; but the moment that the warrior had entered the clearing a loud "Kreeg-ah!" rang out from behind him, immediately followed by a chorus of replies from different directions, as the great bulls crashed through the trees in answer to the summons of their fellow.

The black man halted at the first cry and looked about him. He could see nothing, but he knew the voice of the hairy tree men whom he and his kind feared, not alone because of the strength and ferocity of the savage beings, but as well through a superstitious terror engendered by the manlike appearance of the apes.

But Bulabantu was no coward. He heard the apes all about him; he knew that escape was probably impossible, so he stood his ground, his spear ready in his hand and a war cry trembling on his lips. He would sell his life dearly, would Bulabantu, under-chief of the village of Mbonga, the chief.

Tarzan and Tantor were but a short distance away when the first cry of the sentry rang out through the quiet jungle. Like a flash the ape-man leaped from the elephant's back to a near-by tree and was swing-ing rapidly in the direction of the clearing before the echoes of the first "Kreeg-ah" had died away. When he arrived he saw a dozen bulls circling a single Go-mangani. With a blood-curdling scream Tarzan sprang to the attack. He hated the blacks even more than did the apes, and here was an opportunity for a kill in the open. What had the Gomangani done? Had he slain one of the tribe?

Tarzan asked the nearest ape. No, the Gomangani had harmed none. Gozan, being on watch, had seen him coming through the forest and had warned the tribe—that was all. The ape-man pushed through the circle of bulls, none of which as yet had worked himself into sufficient frenzy for a charge, and came where he had a full and close view of the black. He recognized the man instantly. Only the night before he had seen him facing the eyes in the dark, while his fellows groveled in the dirt at his feet, too terri-fied even to defend themselves. Here was a brave man, and Tarzan had deep admiration for bravery. Even his hatred of the blacks was not so strong a pas-sion as his love of courage. He would have joyed in battling with a black warrior at almost any time; but this one he did not wish to kill—he felt, vaguely, that the man had earned his life by his brave defense of it on the preceding night, nor did he fancy the odds that were pitted against the lone warrior.

He turned to the apes. "Go back to your feeding," he said, "and let this Gomangani go his way in peace. He has not harmed us, and last night I saw him fighting Numa and Sabor with fire, alone in the jungle. He is brave. Why should we kill one who is brave and who has not attacked us? Let him go."

The apes growled. They were displeased. "Kill the Gomangani!" cried one.

"Yes," roared another, "kill the Gomangani and the Tarmangani as well."

"Kill the white ape!" screamed Gozan, "he is no ape at all; but a Gomangani with his skin off."

"Kill Tarzan!" bellowed Gunto. "Kill! Kill! Kill!"

The bulls were now indeed working themselves into the frenzy of slaughter; but against Tarzan rather than the black man. A shaggy form charged through them, hurling those it came in contact with to one side as a strong man might scatter children. It was Taug—great, savage Taug.

"Who says 'kill Tarzan'?" he demanded. "Who kills Tarzan must kill Taug, too. Who can kill Taug? Taug will tear your insides from you and feed them to Dango."

"We can kill you all," replied Gunto. "There are many of us and few of you," and he was right. Tarzan knew that he was right. Taug knew it; but neither would admit such a possibility. It is not the way of bull apes.

"I am Tarzan," cried the ape-man. "I am Tarzan. Mighty hunter; mighty fighter. In all the jungle none so great as Tarzan."

Then, one by one, the opposing bulls recounted their virtues and their prowess. And all the time the combatants came closer and closer to one another. Thus do the bulls work themselves to the proper pitch before engaging in battle.

Gunto came, stiff-legged, close to Tarzan and sniffed at him, with bared fangs. Tarzan rumbled forth a low, menacing growl. They might repeat these tactics a dozen times; but sooner or later one bull would close with another and then the whole hideous pack would be tearing and rending at their prey.

Bulabantu, the black man, had stood wide-eyed in wonder from the moment he had seen Tarzan approaching through the apes. He had heard much of this devil-god who ran with the hairy tree people; but never before had he seen him in full daylight. He knew him well enough from the description of those who had seen him and from the glimpses he had had of the marauder upon several occasions when the ape-man had entered the village of Mbonga, the chief, by night, in the perpetration of one of his numerous ghastly jokes.

Bulabantu could not, of course, understand anything which passed between Tarzan and the apes; but he saw that the ape-man and one of the larger bulls were in argument with the others. He saw that these two were standing with their back toward him and between him and the balance of the tribe, and he guessed, though it seemed improbable, that they might be defending him. He knew that Tarzan had once spared the life of Mbonga, the chief, and that he had succored Tibo, and Tibo's mother, Momaya. So it was not impossible that he would help Bula-bantu; but how he could accomplish it Bulabantu could not guess; nor as a matter of fact could Tarzan, for the odds against him were too great.

Gunto and the others were slowly forcing Tarzan and Taug back toward Bulabantu. The ape-man thought of his words with Tantor just a short time before: "Yes, Tantor, it is good to live. I should hate to die." And now he knew that he was about to die, for the temper of the great bulls was mounting rapidly against him. Always had many of them hated him, and all were suspicious of him. They knew he was different. Tarzan knew it too; but he was glad that he was—he was a MAN; that he had learned from his picture-books, and he was very proud of the distinction. Presently, though, he would be a dead man.

Gunto was preparing to charge. Tarzan knew the signs. He knew that the balance of the bulls would charge with Gunto. Then it would soon be over. Something moved among the verdure at the opposite side of the clearing. Tarzan saw it just as

Gunto, with the terrifying cry of a challenging ape, sprang forward. Tarzan voiced a peculiar call and then crouched to meet the assault. Taug crouched, too, and Bulabantu, assured now that these two were fighting upon his side, couched his spear and sprang between them to receive the first charge of the enemy.

Simultaneously a huge bulk broke into the clearing from the jungle behind the charging bulls. The trumpeting of a mad tusker rose shrill above the cries of the anthropoids, as Tantor, the elephant, dashed swiftly across the clearing to the aid of his friend.

Gunto never closed upon the ape-man, nor did a fang enter flesh upon either side. The terrific reverberation of Tantor's challenge sent the bulls scurrying to the trees, jabbering and scolding. Taug raced off with them. Only Tarzan and Bulabantu remained. The latter stood his ground because he saw that the devil-god did not run, and because the black had the courage to face a certain and horrible death beside one who had quite evidently dared death for him.

But it was a surprised Gomangani who saw the mighty elephant come to a sudden halt in front of the ape-man and caress him with his long, sinuous trunk.

Tarzan turned toward the black man. "Go!" he said in the language of the apes, and pointed in the direction of the village of Mbonga. Bulabantu understood the gesture, if not the word, nor did he lose time in obeying. Tarzan stood watching him until he had disappeared. He knew that the apes would not follow. Then he said to the elephant: "Pick me up!" and the tusker swung him lightly to his head.

"Tarzan goes to his lair by the big water," shouted the ape-man to the apes in the trees. "All of you are more foolish than Manu, except Taug and Teeka. Taug and Teeka may come to see Tarzan; but the others must keep away. Tarzan is done with the tribe of Kerchak."

He prodded Tantor with a calloused toe and the big beast swung off across the clearing, the apes watching them until they were swallowed up by the jungle.

Before the night fell Taug killed Gunto, picking a quarrel with him over his attack upon Tarzan.

For a moon the tribe saw nothing of Tarzan of the Apes. Many of them probably never gave him a thought; but there were those who missed him more than Tarzan imagined. Taug and Teeka often wished that he was back, and Taug determined a dozen times to go and visit Tarzan in his seaside lair; but first one thing and then another interfered.

One night when Taug lay sleepless looking up at the starry heavens he recalled the strange things that Tarzan once had suggested to him—that the bright spots were the eyes of the meat-eaters waiting in the dark of the jungle sky to leap upon Goro, the moon, and devour him. The more he thought about this matter the more perturbed he became.

And then a strange thing happened. Even as Taug looked at Goro, he saw a portion of one edge disappear, precisely as though something was gnawing upon it. Larger and larger became the hole in the side of Goro. With a scream, Taug leaped to his feet. His frenzied "Kreeg-ahs!" brought the terrified tribe screaming and chattering toward him.

"Look!" cried Taug, pointing at the moon. "Look! It is as Tarzan said. Numa has sprung through the fires and is devouring Goro. You called Tarzan names and drove him from the tribe; now see how wise he was. Let one of you who hated Tarzan go to Goro's aid. See the eyes in the dark jungle all about Goro. He is in danger and none can help him—none except Tarzan. Soon Goro will be devoured by Numa and we shall have no more light after Kudu seeks his lair. How shall we dance the Dum-Dum without the light of Goro?"

The apes trembled and whimpered. Any manifestation of the powers of nature always filled them with terror, for they could not understand.

"Go and bring Tarzan," cried one, and then they all took up the cry of "Tarzan!" "Bring Tarzan!" "He will save Goro." But who was to travel the dark jungle by night to fetch him?

"I will go," volunteered Taug, and an instant later he was off through the Stygian gloom toward the little land-locked harbor by the sea.

And as the tribe waited they watched the slow devouring of the moon. Already Numa had eaten out a great semicircular piece. At that rate Goro would be entirely gone before Kudu came again. The apes trembled at the thought of perpetual darkness by night. They could not sleep. Restlessly they moved here and there among the branches of trees, watching Numa of the skies at his deadly feast, and listening for the coming of Taug with Tarzan.

Goro was nearly gone when the apes heard the sounds of the approach through the trees of the two they awaited, and presently Tarzan, followed by Taug, swung into a near-by tree.

The ape-man wasted no time in idle words. In his hand was his long bow and at his back hung a quiver full of arrows, poisoned arrows that he had stolen from the village of the blacks; just as he had stolen the bow. Up into a great tree he clambered, higher and higher until he stood swaying upon a small limb which bent low beneath his weight. Here he had a clear and unobstructed view of the heavens. He saw Goro and the inroads which the hungry Numa had made into his shining surface.

Raising his face to the moon, Tarzan shrilled forth his hideous challenge. Faintly and from afar came the roar of an answering lion. The apes shivered. Numa of the skies had answered Tarzan.

Then the ape-man fitted an arrow to his bow, and drawing the shaft back, aimed its point at the heart of Numa where he lay in the heavens devouring Goro. There was a loud twang as the released bolt shot into the dark heavens. Again and again did Tarzan of the Apes launch his arrows at Numa, and all the while the apes of the tribe of Kerchak huddled together in terror.

At last came a cry from Taug. "Look! Look!" he screamed. "Numa is killed. Tarzan has killed Numa. See! Goro is emerging from the belly of Numa," and, sure enough, the moon was gradually emerging from whatever had devoured her, whether it was Numa, the lion, or the shadow of the earth; but were you to try to convince an ape of the tribe of Kerchak that it was aught but Numa who so nearly devoured Goro that night, or that another than Tarzan preserved the brilliant god of their savage and mysterious rites from a frightful death, you would have difficulty—and a fight on your hands.

And so Tarzan of the Apes came back to the tribe of Kerchak, and in his coming he took a long stride toward the kingship, which he ultimately won, for now the apes looked up to him as a superior being.

In all the tribe there was but one who was at all skeptical about the plausibility of Tarzan's remarkable rescue of Goro, and that one, strange as it may seem, was Tarzan of the Apes.

Zorro

[JOHNSTON McCULLEY]

DON DIEGO FEELS ILL

One hour after Don Carlos Pulido and his ladies had been incarcerated in the *carcel*, Don Diego Vega, dressed most fastidiously, made his way slowly on foot up the slope to the *presidio* to make his call on his excellency, the governor.

He walked with swinging stride, gazing both to right and left as if at the hills in the distance, and once he stopped to observe a blossom that bloomed beside the path. His rapier was at his side, his most fashionable one with its jeweled hilt, and in his right hand he carried a handkerchief of flimsy lace, which he wafted this way and that like a dandy, and now and then touched it to the tip of his nose.

He bowed ceremoniously to two or three *caballeros* who passed him, but spoke to none beyond the necessary words of greeting, and they did not seek conversation with him. For, remembering that they had thought Don Diego Vega was courting the daughter of Don Carlos, they wondered how he would take the matter of her imprisonment along with her father and mother. They did not care to discuss the matter, for their own feelings were high, and they feared they might be betrayed into utterances that might be termed treasonable.

Don Diego came to the front door of the *presidio*, and the sergeant in charge called the soldiers to attention, giving Vega the salute due his station in life. Don Diego answered it with a wave of his hand and a smile, and went on to the *commandante's* office, where the governor was receiving such *caballeros* as cared to call and express their loyalty.

He greeted his excellency with carefully chosen words, bowed over his hand, and then took the chair the governor was kind enough to indicate.

"Don Diego Vega," the governor said, "I am doubly glad that you have called upon me to-day, for in these times a man who holds high office would know his friends."

"I should have called sooner, but I was away from my house at the time you arrived," Don Diego said.

"You contemplate remaining here long in Reina de Los Angeles, excellency?"

"Until this highwayman, known as Señor Zorro, is either slain or taken," the governor said.

"By the saints! Am I never to hear the last of that rogue?" Don Diego cried. "I have heard of nothing else for these many days. I go to spend an evening with a *fray*, and in comes a crowd of soldiers chasing this Señor Zorro. I repair to the *hacienda* of my father to get me peace and quiet, and along comes a crowd of *caballeros* seeking news of Señor Zorro.

"These be turbulent times! A man whose nature inclines him to music and the poets has no right to exist in the present age!"

"It desolates me that you have been annoyed," the governor said, laughing. "But I hope to have the fellow soon, and so put an end to that particular annoyance. Captain Ramón has sent for his big sergeant and his troopers to return. I brought an escort of twenty. And so we have ample men to run down this Curse of Capistrano when next he makes his appearance."

"Let us hope it will end as it should," said Don Diego.

"A man in high office has many things with which to contend," the governor went on. "Look at what I was forced to do this day! I am called upon to put in prison a man of good blood, and his lady wife and tender daughter. But the state must be protected."

"I suppose you mean Don Carlos Pulido and his family?"

"I do, *caballero*."

"Now that it is called to my mind again, I must say a few words regarding that," Don Diego said. "I am not sure that my honor is not involved."

"Why, *caballero*, how can that be?"

"My father has ordered that I get me a wife and set up my establishment properly. Some days ago I requested of Don Carlos Pulido permission to pay my addresses to his daughter."

"Ha! I understand! But you are not the betrothed of the young lady?"

"Not yet, excellency."

"Then your honor is not involved, Don Diego, that I can see."

"But I have been paying court to her."

"You may thank the saints that it has gone no further, Don Diego. Think how it would look if you were allied with this family now! As for getting you a wife—come north with me to San Francisco de Asis, *caballero*, where the *señoritas* are far more lovely than here in your southland.

"Look over those of good blood, and let me know your preference, and I'll guarantee that the lady will listen to your suit and accept your hand

and name. And I can guarantee, also, that she will be of a loyal family with which it will be no shame to make a contract. We shall get you a wife of the proper sort, *caballero*."

"If you will pardon me, is it not taking stern measures to have Don Carlos and his ladies thrown into the *carcel*?" Don Diego asked, flicking dust from his sleeve.

"I find it necessary, *señor*."

"Do you think it will add to your popularity, excellency?"

"Whether it does or not, the state must be served."

"Men of good blood hate to see such a thing, and there may be murmurings," Don Diego warned. "I should hate to see your excellency make a wrong step at this juncture."

"What would you have me do?" the governor asked.

"Place Don Carlos and the ladies under arrest, if you will, but do not incarcerate them. It is unnecessary; they will not run away. Bring them to trial as gentle folk should be brought to trial."

"You are bold, *caballero*."

"By the saints, am I talking too much?"

"It were better to leave these matters to the few of us who are trusted with attention to them," the governor said. "I can understand, of course, how it irks a man of good blood to see a don thrown into a *carcel*, and to see his ladies treated likewise, but in such a case as this—"

"I have not heard the nature of the case," Don Diego said.

"Ha! Perhaps you may change your mind when you learn it. You have been speaking of this Señor Zorro. What if I tell you that the highwayman is being shielded and protected and fed by Don Carlos Pulido?"

"That is astonishing!"

"And that the Doña Catalina is a party to the treason? And that the lovely *señorita* has seen fit to talk treasonably and dip her pretty hands into a conspiracy against the state?"

"This is past belief!" Don Diego cried.

"Some nights ago Señor Zorro was at the Pulido *hacienda*. Warning was fetched the *comandante* by a native who is loyal. Don Carlos aided the bandit in tricking the soldiers, hid him in a closet, and when Captain Ramón was there alone, this highwayman stepped from the closet and attacked him treacherously and wounded him."

"By the saints!"

"And while you were gone and the Pulidos were your house guests, *señor*, Señor Zorro was in your house, speaking to the *señorita*, when the *comandante* walked in upon them. And the *señorita* grasped

Captain Ramon by the arm and annoyed him until this Señor Zorro had made good his escape!"

"It is past comprehension!" Don Diego exclaimed.

"Captain Ramon has placed before me a hundred such items of suspicion. Can you wonder now that I had them placed in *carcel*? Did I merely have them put under arrest, this Señor Zorro would combine forces with them and aid them to escape."

"And your intensions, excellency?"

"I shall keep them in *carcel* while my troopers run down this highwayman. I shall force him to confess and implicate them—and then they shall have a trial."

"These turbulent times!" Don Diego complained.

"As a loyal man—and I hope an admirer of mine—you should hope to see foes of the state confounded."

"I do! Most sincerely do I! All real foes of the state should receive punishment."

"I am joyed to hear you say that, *caballero*!" the governor cried, and he reached across the table and grasped Don Diego fervently by the hand.

There was some more talk that amounted to nothing, and then Don Diego took his leave, for there were other men waiting to see the governor. After he had left the office the governor looked across at Captain Ramon and smiled.

"You are right, *comandante*," he said. "Such a man could not be a traitor. It would tire him too much to think treasonable thoughts. What a man! He must be enough to drive that old fire-eater of a father of his insane!"

Don Diego made his way slowly down the hill, greeting those he passed, and stopping again to regard the little flowers that blossomed by the wayside. At the corner of the plaza he met a young *caballero* who was glad to call him friend, one of the small band of men who had spent the night at Don Alejandro's *hacienda*.

"Ha! Don Diego, a fair day to you!" he cried. And then he lowered his voice and stepped nearer: "Has, by any chance, the man we call leader of our league of avengers, sent you a message this day?"

"By the bright blue sky—no!" Don Diego said. "Why should the man?"

"This Pulido business. It seems an outrage. Some of us have been wondering whether our leader does not intend to take a hand in it. We have been anticipating a message."

"By the saints! Oh, I trust not!" Don Diego said. "I could not endure an adventure of any sort to-night. I—er—my head aches, and I fear I am going to have a fever. I shall have to see an apothecary about it. There are shiverings up and down my spine, also. Is not that a symptom? During the *siesta* hour I was bothered with a pain in my left leg just above the knee. It must be the weather!"

"Let us hope that it will not result seriously," laughed his friend, and hurried on across the plaza.

THE SIGN OF THE FOX

An hour after dusk that night a native sought out one of the *caballeros* with the intelligence that a gentleman wished to speak to him immediately, and that this gentleman was evidently wealthy since he had given the native a coin for carrying the message, when he might just as well have given nothing more than a cuff alongside the head; also that the mysterious gentleman would be waiting along the path that ran toward the San Gabriel trail, and to be sure that the *caballero* would come he had bade the native say that there was a fox in the neighborhood.

"A fox! Zorro—fox!" the *caballero* thought, and then he ruined the native forever by giving him another coin.

He went to the rendezvous immediately, and there he found Señor Zorro sitting his big horse, his face masked, the cloak wrapped around his body.

"You will pass the word, *caballero*," Señor Zorro said. "I would have all men who are loyal and wish to do so, meet at midnight in the little valley beyond the hill. You know the place? *Si?* I shall be waiting."

Then Señor Zorro wheeled his horse and dashed away in the darkness, and the *caballero* went back to the *pueblo* and passed the word to those men he knew could be depended upon, and urged upon them that they pass it to others of the league. One went to Don Diego's house, but was told by the *despensero* that Don Diego had complained of a fever and had retired to his chamber, and had left word that he would flay alive any servant who dared enter the room unless he called.

Near the hour of midnight the *caballeros* began slipping from the *pueblo* one at a time, each upon the back of his best horse, and each armed with sword and pistol. Each man had a mask that could be put over his features instantly, for that had been decided upon at Don Alejandro's *hacienda*, among other things.

The *pueblo* was in darkness, save that there were lights in the tavern, where some of his excellency's escort made merry with the local troopers. For Sergeant Pedro Gonzales had returned with his men just before nightfall, glad to be back from a fruitless chase, and hoping that the next scent would be warmer.

Those in the tavern had gone down the hill from the *presidio*, some leaving their horses there without saddles or bridles on, and they had no thought of an encounter with Señor Zorro this night. The fat landlord was kept busy, for the soldiers from the north had coins in their purses and were willing to spend them. Sergeant Gonzales, holding the attention of the company as usual, was detailing at length what he would do to this Señor Zorro if the saints were kind enough to let them meet and grant him his blade in his hand.

There were lights in the big lounging-room of the *presidio*, too, for few of the soldiers had retired. And there were lights in the house where his excellency was a guest, but the remainder of the *pueblo* was in darkness, and the people slept.

In the *carcel* there was no light at all except one candle burning in the office, where a sleepy man was on guard. The jailer was in his bed. Prisoners moaned on the hard benches in the prison-room. Don Carlos Pulido stood before a window, looking up at the stars; and his wife and daughter huddled on a bench beside him, unable to sleep in such surroundings.

The *caballeros* found Señor Zorro waiting for them as he had said he would be, but he remained aloof, speaking scarcely a word, until all were present.

"Are all here?" he asked then.

"All except Don Diego Vega," one replied. "He is ill with a fever, *señor*."

And all the *caballeros* chuckled, for they had an idea the fever was caused by cowardice.

"I take it that you know something of what is in my mind," Señor Zorro said. "We know what has happened to Don Carlos Pulido and the ladies of

his family. We know they are innocent of any treason; and were they not, they should have not been
taken to *carcel* and incarcerated with common felons
and drunkards.

"Think of those gentle ladies in such surroundings! Think of it—because Don Carlos has the ill
will of the governor! It is the sense of the league
that something be done in this matter? If it is not,
then will I do something by myself!"

"Rescue them!" a *caballero* said; and the others
growled their approval. Here was a chance for risk
and adventure and an opportunity to do a good deed.

"We must enter the *pueblo* quietly," *Señor* Zorro
said. "There is no moon, and we will not be observed if we use caution. We shall approach the *carcel*
from the south. Each man will have his task to do.

"Some will surround the building to give notice
if any approach it. Others must be ready to beat off
the soldiers, if they respond to an alarm. Others will
effect an entrance to the *carcel* with me, and rescue
the prisoners."

"It is an excellent plan," one said.

"That is bust a small part of it. Don Carlos is a
proud man, and if given time for reflection may refuse to be rescued. We cannot allow that. Certain
ones will seize him and take him from the place.
Others will attend to the Doña Catalina. I will

undertake to care for the *señorita*. Now—we have
them free! And then what?"

He heard murmurs, but no distinct reply, and so
he continued to outline the plan.

"All will ride to the highway just below this
place," he said. "At that point we shall scatter. Those
who have the Doña Catalina in charge will hasten
with her to the *hacienda* of Don Alejandro Vega,
where she can be hidden if necessary, and where the
governor's soldiers will hesitate before entering and
seizing her.

"Those who have Don Carlos in charge will take
the road to Pala, and at a certain point some ten
miles from this *pueblo* they will be met by two natives of understanding, who will give the sign of the
fox. The natives will take Don Carlos in charge and
care for him.

"When these things are done, each *caballero* will
ride to his home quietly and alone, telling what
story pleases him, and using great caution. I shall
have conducted the *señorita* to a safe place by that
time. She shall be given into the keeping of old Fray
Felipe, a man we can trust, and he will hide her if
he must. Then we will watch to see what the governor does."

"What can he do?" a *caballero* asked. "Have them
searched for, of course."

"We must await developments," Señor Zorro said. "Are all now ready?"

They assured him that they were, and so he named the men for each task, and then they left the little valley and rode slowly and cautiously around the little town, and approached it from the south.

They heard the soldiers shouting and singing in the tavern, saw the lights in the *presidio*, and crept toward the *carcel* quietly, riding two by two.

In a short time it had been surrounded by quiet, determined men; and then Señor Zorro and four others dismounted and went to the door of the building.

THE RESCUE

Señor Zorro knocked upon it with the hilt of his sword. They heard a man gasp inside, presently heard his steps on the stone flooring, and after a little time light showed through the cracks, and the aperture was opened, and the sleepy face of the guard appeared.

"What is wanted?" he asked.

Señor Zorro thrust the muzzle of his pistol through the aperture and into the man's face, and in such fashion that the little door could not be closed.

"Open, if you value your life! Open—and make not the slightest sound!" Señor Zorro commanded.

"What—what is this?"

"Señor Zorro is talking to you!"

"By the saints—"

"Open, fool, or you die instantly!"

"I—I'll open the door. Do not shoot, good Señor Zorro! I am only a poor guard and not a fighting man! I pray you do not shoot!"

"Open quickly!"

"As soon as I can fit the key to lock, good Señor Zorro!"

They heard him rattling the keys; presently one was turned in the lock, and the heavy door was thrown open.

Señor Zorro and his four companions rushed inside, and slammed and fastened the door again. The guard found the muzzle of a pistol pressed against the side of his head, and would have knelt before these five masked and terrible men, only one of them caught him by the hair and held him up.

"Where sleeps the keeper of this infernal hole?" Señor Zorro demanded.

"In yonder room, *señor!*"

"And where have you put Don Carlos Pulido and his ladies?"

"In the common prison-room, *señor!*"

Señor Zorro motioned to the others, strode across the room, and threw open the door to the jailer's chamber. The man already was sitting up in bed, having heard the sounds in the other room, and he blinked in fright when he beheld the highwayman by the light of the candle.

"Do not make a move *señor*!" Zorro warned. "One screech, and you are a dead man! Señor Zorro confronts you!"

"May the saints preserve me—"

"Where are the keys to the prison rooms?"

"On—on that table, *señor*."

Señor Zorro picked them up, and then whirled upon the jailer again and rushed toward him.

"Lie down!" he commanded. "On your face, scoundrel!"

Señor Zorro tore strips from a blanket, and bound the jailers hands and feet, and made a gag which he affixed.

"To escape death," he said, then, "it is necessary for you to remain exactly as you are now, without making a sound, for some time after we have left the *carcel*. I shall leave it to your own judgment to decide the length of time."

Then he hurried back into the main office, beckoned the others, and led the way down the evil-smelling hall.

"Which door?" he asked of the guard.

"The second one, *señor*."

They hurried to it, and Señor Zorro unlocked it and threw it open. He forced the guard to hold a candle high above his head.

A gasp of pity came from beneath the highway-man's mask. He saw the aged don standing by the window, saw the two women crouched on the bench, saw the vile companions they had in this miserable place.

"Now may Heaven forgive the governor!" he cried.

Señorita Lolita looked up in alarm, and then gave a glad cry. Don Carlos whirled at the highwayman's words.

"Señor Zorro!" he gasped.

"The same, Don Carlos! I have come with some friends to rescue you!"

"I cannot allow it, *señor*. I shall not run away from what is in store for me. And it would avail me little to have you do the rescuing. I am accused now of harboring you, I understand. How ill it look, then, if you effect my escape?"

"There is no time for argument," Señor Zorro said. "I am not alone in this, but have twenty-six men with me. And a man of your blood, and gentle ladies such as those of your family, shall not spend an entire night in this miserable hole if we can prevent it. *Caballeros!*"

The last word was one of command. Two of the *caballeros* threw themselves upon Don Carlos, subdued him quickly, and half carried him into the hall and along it toward the office. Two others grasped the Doña Catalina by the arms, as gently as they could, and so carried her along.

Señor Zorro bowed before the *señorita*, and extended a hand, which she clasped gladly.

"You must trust me, *señorita*," he said.

"To love is to trust, *señor*!"

"All things have been arranged. Ask no questions, but do as I bid. Come!"

He threw an arm around her, and so led her from the prison-room, leaving the door open behind him. If some of the miserable wretches there could win through and out of the building, Señor Zorro had no wish to prevent them. More than half of them, he judged, were there because of prejudice or injustice.

Don Carlos was causing an unearthly clamor, shouting that he refused to be rescued, and that he would stay and face the governor at the trial, and show the blood that was in him. Doña Catalina was whimpering a bit because of fright, but made no resistance.

They reached the office, and Señor Zorro ordered the guard to a corner of it, with instructions to remain there quietly for some time after they had gone. And then one of the *caballeros* threw open the outside door.

There was a tumult outside at that moment. Two soldiers had approached with a fellow caught stealing at the tavern, and the *caballeros* had stopped them. One glance at the masked faces had been enough to tell the troopers that here was something wrong.

A soldier fired a pistol, and a *caballero* answered the fire, neither hitting the mark. But the shooting was enough to attract the attention of those in the tavern, and also of the guards at the *presidio*.

Troopers at the *presidio* were awakened immediately, and took the places of the guards while the latter mounted and spurred down the hill to ascertain the cause of the sudden tumult at that hour of the night. Sergeant Pedro Gonzales and others hurried from the tavern. Señor Zorro and his companions found themselves facing a resistance when they least expected it.

The jailer had gathered courage enough to work himself free of gag and bonds, and he shrieked through a window of his chamber that prisoners were being rescued by Señor Zorro. His shriek was understood by Sergeant Gonzales, who screeched for his men to follow him and earn a part of his excellency's reward.

But the *caballeros* had their three rescued prisoners on horseback, and they spurred through the gathering throng and so dashed across the plaza and toward the highway.

Shots flew about them, but no man was hit. Don Carlos Pulido was still screaming that he refused to be rescued. Doña Catalina had fainted, for which the *caballero* who had her in charge was grateful, since he could give more attention to his horse and weapons.

Señor Zorro rode wildly, with the Señorita Lolita in the saddle before him. He spurred his magnificent horse ahead of all the others, and so led the way to the highroad. And when he had reached it, he pulled up his mount and watched the others come galloping to the spot, to ascertain whether there had been casualties.

"Carry out your orders, *caballeros!*" he commanded, when he saw that all had won through safely.

And so the band was broken into three detachments. One rushing along the Pala Road with Don Carlos. Another took the highway that would lead them to the *hacienda* of Don Alejandro. Señor Zorro, riding without any of his comrades at his side, galloped toward Fray Felipe's place, the *señorita's* arms clasped tightly about his neck and the *señorita's* voice in his ear.

"I knew that you would come for me, *señor,*" she said. "I knew you were a true man and would not see me and my parents remain in that miserable place."

Señor Zorro did not answer her with words, for it was not a time for speech with his enemies so close at his heels, but his arms pressed the *señorita* closer to him.

He had reached the crest of the first hill; and now he stopped the horse to listen for sounds of pursuit, and to watch the flickering lights far behind.

For there was a multitude of lights in the plaza now, and in all the houses, for the *pueblo* had been aroused. The *presidio* building was ablaze with light, and he could hear a trumpet being blown, and knew that every available trooper would be sent on the chase.

The sound of galloping horses came to his ears. The troopers knew in what direction the rescuers had traveled; and the pursuit would be swift and relentless, with his excellency on the scene to offer fabulous rewards and urge on his men with promises of good posts and promotion.

But one thing pleased Señor Zorro as his horse galloped down the dusty highway and the *señorita* clung to him and the keen wind cut his face—he knew that the pursuit would have to be divided into three parties.

He pressed the *señorita* to him again, put spurs to his horse, and rode furiously through the night.

CLOSE QUARTERS

Over the hills peeped the moon.

Señor Zorro would have had the sky heavy with clouds this night and the moon obscured, could he have had things his own way, for now he was riding along the upper trail, and his pursuers were close behind and could see him against the brightening sky.

The horses ridden by the troopers were fresh, too, and the most of those belonging to the men of his excellency's escort were magnificent beasts as swift as any in the country, and able to endure many miles of travel at a terrific pace.

But now the highwayman thought only of getting all the speed possible out of his own mount, and of making as great as he could the distance between himself and those who followed; for at the end of his journey he would need quite a little time, if he was to accomplish what he had set out to do.

He bent low over the *señorita*, and felt his horse with the reins, making himself almost a part of the animal he rode, as any good horseman can. He reached the crest of another hill, and glanced back before he began the descent into the valley. He could see the foremost of his pursuers.

Had Señor Zorro been alone, no doubt the situation would have caused him no uneasiness, for many times he had been in a position more difficult, and had escaped. But the *señorita* was on the saddle before him now, and he wanted to get her to a place of safety, not only because she was the *señorita* and the woman he loved, but also because he was not the sort of man to let a prisoner he had rescued be recaptured. Such an event, he felt, would be a reflection on his skill and daring.

Mile after mile he rode, the *señorita* clinging to him, and neither speaking a word. Señor Zorro knew that he had gained some on those who followed, but not enough to suit his purpose.

Now he urged his horse to greater effort and they flew along the dusty highway, past *haciendas* where the hounds barked in sudden alarm, past the huts of natives where the clamor of beating hoofs on the hard road caused bronze men and women to tumble from their bunks and rush to their doors.

Once he charged through a flock of sheep that were being driven to Reina de Los Angeles and the market there, and scattered them to either side of the road, leaving cursing herders behind him. The herders gathered the flock again, just in time to have the pursuing soldiers scatter it once more.

On and on he rode, until he could see, far ahead, the mission buildings at San Gabriel glistening in the moonlight. He came to a fork in the road, and took the trail that ran to the right, toward the *hacienda* of Fray Felipe.

Señor Zorro was a reader of men, and he was trusting to his judgment to-night. He had known that the Señorita Lolita would have to be left either where there were women, else where there was a robed Franciscan to stand guard over her, for Señor Zorro was determined to protect his lady's good name. And so he was pinning his faith to old Fray Felipe.

Now the horse was galloping over softer ground, and was not making such good speed. Señor Zorro had little hope that the troopers would turn into the San Gabriel Road when they arrived at the fork, as they might have done had it not been moonlight and they had been unable to catch sight now and then of the man they pursued. He was within a mile of Fray Felipe's *hacienda* now, and once more he gave his horse the spurs in an effort to obtain greater speed.

"I shall have scant time, *señorita*," he said, bending over her and speaking into her ear. "Everything may depend upon whether I have been able to judge a man correctly. I ask only that you trust me."

"You know I do that, *señor!*"

"And you must trust the man to whom I am carrying you, *señorita*, and listen well to his advice upon all matters concerned with this adventure. The man is a *fray*."

"Then everything will be well, *señor*," she replied, clinging to him closely.

"If the saints are kind, we shall meet again soon, *señorita*. I shall count the hours, and deem each one of them an age. I believe there are happier days ahead for us."

"May Heaven grant it!" the girl breathed.

"Where there is love, there may be hope, *señorita*."

"Then my hope is great, *señor*."

"And mine!" he said.

He turned his horse into Fray Felipe's driveway now, and dashed toward the house. His intention was to stop only long enough to leave the girl, hoping that Fray Felipe would afford her protection, and then ride on, making considerable noise and drawing the troopers after him. He wanted them to think that he was merely taking a short cut across Fray Felipe's land to the other road, and that he had not stopped at the house.

He reined in his horse before the veranda steps, sprang to the ground and lifted the *señorita* from the saddle, hurrying with her to the door. He beat against it with his fist, praying that Fray Felipe was a light sleeper and easily aroused. From the far distance there came a low drumming sound that he knew was made by the hoofs of his pursuers' horses.

It seemed to Señor Zorro that it was an age before the old *fray* threw open the door and stood framed in it, holding a candle in one hand. The highwayman stepped in swiftly and closed the door behind him, so no light would show outside. Fray Felipe had taken a step backward in astonishment when he had beheld the masked man and the *señorita* he escorted.

"I am Señor Zorro, *fray*," the highwayman said, speaking swiftly and in low tones. "Perhaps you may feel that you owe me a small debt for certain things?"

"For punishing those who oppressed and mistreated me, I owe you a large debt, *caballero*, though it is against my principles to countenance violence of any sort," Fray Felipe replied.

"I was sure that I had made no mistake in reading your character," Señor Zorro went on. "This *señorita* is Lolita, the only daughter of Don Carlos Pulido."

"Ha!"

"Don Carlos is a friend of the *frailes*, as you well know, and has known oppression and persecution the same as they. To-day the governor came to Reina de Los Angeles and had Don Carlos arrested and thrown into the *carcel* on a charge that has no true worth, as I happen to know. He also had the Doña Catalina and this young lady put in *carcel*, in the same prison-room with drunkards and dissolute women. With the aid of some good friends, I rescued them."

"May the saints bless you, *señor*, for that kind of action!" Fray Felipe cried.

"Troopers are pursuing us, *fray*. It is not seemly, of course, that the *señorita* ride farther with me alone. Do you take her and hide her, *fray*—unless you fear that such a course may cause you grave trouble."

"*Señor!*" Fray Felipe thundered.

"If the soldiers take her, they will put her in *carcel* again, and probably she will be mistreated. Care for her, then, protect her, and you will more than discharge any obligation you may feel that you owe me."

"And you, *señor?*"

"I shall ride on, that the troopers may pursue me and not stop here at your house. I shall communicate with you later, *fray*. It is agreed between us?"

"It is agreed!" Fray Felipe replied solemnly. "And I would clasp you by the hand, *señor!*"

That handclasp was short, yet full of expression for all that. Señor Zorro then whirled toward the door.

"Blow out your candle!" he directed. "They must see no light when I open the door."

In an instant Fray Felipe had complied, and they were in darkness. Señorita Lolita felt Señor Zorro's lips press against her own for an instant, and knew that he had raised the bottom of his mask to give her this caress. And then she felt one of Fray Felipe's strong arms around her.

"Be of good courage, daughter," the *fray* said. "Señor Zorro, it appears, has as many lives as a cat, and something tells me he was not born to be slain by troopers of his excellency."

The highwayman laughed lightly at that, opened the door and darted through, closed it softly behind him, and so was gone.

Great eucalyptus-trees shrouded the front of the house in shadows, and in the midst of these shadows was Señor Zorro's horse. He noticed, as he ran toward the beast, that the soldiers were galloping down the driveway, that they were much nearer than he had expected to find them when he emerged from the house.

He ran quickly toward his mount, tripped on a stone and fell, and frightened the animal so that it reared and darted half a dozen paces away, and into the full moonlight.

The foremost of his pursuers shouted when he saw the horse, and dashed toward it. Señor Zorro picked himself up, gave a quick spring, caught the reins from the ground and vaulted into the saddle.

But they were upon him now, surrounding him, their blades flashing in the moonlight. He heard the raucous voice of Sergeant Gonzales ordering the men.

"Alive, if you can, soldiers! His excellency would see the rogue suffer for his crimes. At him, troopers! By the saints!"

Señor Zorro parried a stroke with difficulty, and found himself unhorsed. On foot, he fought his way back into the shadows, and the troopers charged after him. With his back to the bole of a tree, Señor Zorro fought them off.

Three sprang from their saddles to rush in at him. He darted from the tree to another, but could not reach his horse. But one belonging to a dismounted trooper was near him, and he vaulted into the saddle and dashed down the slope toward the barns and corral.

"After the rogue!" he heard Sergeant Gonzales shouting. "His excellency will have us flayed alive if this pretty highwayman escapes us now!"

They charged after him, eager to win promotion and the reward. But Señor Zorro had some sort of a start of them, enough to enable him to play a trick. As he came into the shadow cast by a big barn, he slipped from the saddle, at the same time giving the hose he rode a cut with his rowels. The animal plunged ahead, snorting with pain and fright, running swiftly through the darkness toward the corral below. The soldiers dashed by in pursuit.

Señor Zorro waited until they were past, and then he ran rapidly up the hill again. But he saw that some of the troopers had remained behind to guard the house, evidently with the intention of searching it later, and so he found he could not reach his horse.

And once more there rang out that peculiar cry, half shriek and half moan, with which Señor Zorro had startled those at the *hacienda* of Don Carlos Pulido. His horse raised its head, whinnied once in answer to his call, and galloped toward him.

Señor Zorro was in the saddle in an instant, spurring across a field directly in front of him. His horse went over a stone fence as if it had not been in the way. And after him speedily came a part of the troopers.

They had discovered the trick he had used. They charged at him from both sides, met behind him, followed and strained to cut down his lead. He could hear Sergeant Pedro Gonzales shouting lustily for them to make a capture in the name of the governor.

He hoped that he had drawn them all away from Fray Felipe's house, but he was not sure, and the thing that demanded his attention the most now was the matter of his own escape.

He urged his horse cruelly, knowing that this journey across plowed ground was taking the animal's strength. He longed for a hard trail, the broad highway.

And finally he reached the latter. Now he turned his horse's head toward Reina de Los Angeles, for he had work to do there. There was no *señorita* before him on the saddle now, and the horse felt the difference.

Señor Zorro glanced behind, and exulted to find that he was running away from the soldiers. Over the next hill, and he would be able to elude them!

But he had to be on guard, of course, for there might be troopers in front of him, too. His excellency might have sent reinforcements to Sergeant Gonzales, or might have men watching from the tops of the hills.

He glanced at the sky, and saw that the moon was about to disappear behind a bank of clouds. He would have to make use of the short period of darkness, he knew.

Down into the little valley he rode, and looked back to find that his pursuers were only at the crest of the hill. Then came the darkness, and at the proper time. Señor Zorro had a lead of half a mile on the pursuing soldiers now, but it was not his intention to allow them to chase him into the *pueblo*.

He had friends in this locality. Beside the highway was an adobe hut, where there lived a native Señor Zorro had saved from a beating. Now he dismounted before the hut, and kicked against the door. The frightened native opened it.

"I am pursued," Señor Zorro said.

That appeared to be all that was necessary, for the native immediately threw the door of the hut open wider. Señor Zorro led his horse inside, almost filling the crude building, and the door was hastily shut again.

Behind it, the highwayman and the native stood listening, the former with pistol in one hand and his naked blade in the other.

FLIGHT AND PURSUIT

That the determined pursuit of Señor Zorro and his band of *caballeros* from the *carcel* had been taken up so quickly was due to Sergeant Pedro Gonzales.

Sergeant Gonzales had heard the shots, and had rushed from the tavern with the other troopers at his heels, glad of an excuse to escape without paying for the wine he had ordered. He had heard the shout of the jailer, and had understood it, and immediately had grasped the situation.

"Señor Zorro is rescuing the prisoners!" he screeched. "The highwayman is in our midst again! To horse, troopers, and after him! There is a reward—"

They knew all about the reward, especially the members of the governor's bodyguard, who had heard his excellency rave at the mention of the highwayman's name and declare he would make a captain of the trooper who had captured him or brought in his carcass.

They rushed for their horses, swung themselves into their saddles, and dashed across the plaza toward the *carcel* with Sergeant Gonzales at their head.

They saw the masked *caballeros* galloping across the plaza, and Sergeant Gonzales rubbed his eyes with the back of one hand and swore softly that he had been taking too much wine. He had lied to soften about Señor Zorro having a band of men at his back, that here was the band materialized out of his falsehoods.

When the *caballeros* split into three detachments, Sergeant Gonzales and his troopers were so near them that they observed the maneuver. Gonzales quickly made three troops of the men who followed him, and sent a troop after each band.

He saw the leader of the *caballeros* turn toward San Gabriel, he recognized the leap of the great horse the highwayman rode, and he took after Señor Zorro with an exultant heart, being of a mind to capture or slay the highwayman rather than to re-take any of the rescued prisoners. For Sergeant Pedro Gonzales had not forgotten the time Señor Zorro had played with him in the tavern at Reina de Los Angeles, nor had he given up the idea of tak-ing his vengeance for it.

He had seen Señor Zorro's horse run before, and he wondered a bit now because the highwayman was not putting greater distance between himself and his pursuers. And Sergeant Gonzales guessed the rea-son—that Señor Zorro had Señorita Lolita Pulido on the saddle before him and was carrying her away.

Gonzales was in the lead, and now and then he turned his head and shouted orders and encourage-ment to his troopers. The miles flew beneath them, and Gonzales was glad because he was keeping Señor Zorro in sight.

"To Fray Felipe's—that is where he is riding!" Gonzales told himself. "I knew that old *fray* was in league with the bandit! In some manner he tricked me when I sought this Señor Zorro at his *ha-cienda* before. Perhaps this highwayman has a clever hiding-place there. Ha! By the saints, I shall not be tricked again!"

On they rode, now and then catching glimpses of the man they pursued, and always in the minds of Gonzales and his troopers were thoughts of the reward and promotion a capture would mean. Their horses were beginning to show some fatigue already, but they did not spare the animals.

They saw Señor Zorro turn into the driveway that led to Fray Felipe's house; and Sergeant Gonzales chuckled low down in his throat because he felt that he had guessed correctly.

He had the highwayman now! If Señor Zorro continued to ride, he could be seen and followed because of the bright moonlight; if he stopped, Señor Zorro could not hope to cope successfully with half a score of troopers with Gonzales at their head.

They dashed up to the front of the house and started to surround it. They saw Señor Zorro's horse. And then they saw the highwayman himself, and Gonzales cursed because half a dozen troopers were between him and his prey, and were at him with their swords, threatening to end the business before Gonzales could reach the scene.

He tried to force his horse into the fight. He saw Señor Zorro spring into a saddle and dash away, and the troopers after him. Gonzales, not being close, gave his attention to the other half of his duty—he bade some of his soldiers surround the house so that none could leave it.

Then he saw Señor Zorro take the stone fence, and started in pursuit, all except the guards around the house joining him. But Sergeant Gonzales went only as far as the crest of the first hill. He noticed how the highwayman's horse was running, and realized that he could not be overtaken. Perhaps the sergeant could gain some glory if he returned to Fray Felipe's house and recaptured the *señorita*.

The house was still being guarded when he dismounted before it, and his men reported that none had attempted to leave the building. He called two of his men to his side, and knocked on the door. Almost instantly, it was opened by Fray Felipe.

"Are you just from bed, *fray*?" Gonzales asked.

"Is it not a time of night for honest men to be abed?" Fray Felipe asked in turn.

"It is, *fray*—yet we find you out of it. How does it happen that you have not come from the house before? Did we not make enough noise to awaken you?"

"I heard sounds of combat—"

"And you may hear more, *fray*, else feel the sting of a whip again, unless you answer questions swiftly and to the point. Do you deny that Señor Zorro has been here?"

"I do not."

"Ha! Now we have it! You admit, then, that you are in league with this pretty highwayman, that you shield him upon occasion? You admit that, *fray*?"

"I admit nothing of the sort!" Fray Felipe replied. "I never set my eyes on this Señor Zorro, to my knowledge, until a very few minutes ago."

"That is a likely story! Tell it to the stupid natives! But do not try to tell it to a wise trooper, *fray*! What did this Señor Zorro wish?"

"You were so close upon the man's heels, *señor*, that he scare had time to wish for anything," Fray Felipe said.

"Yet you had some speech with him?"

"I opened the door at his knock, *señor*, the same as I opened it at yours."

"What said he?"

"That soldiers were pursuing him."

"And he asked that you hide him, so he could escape capture at our hands?"

"He did not."

"Wanted a fresh horse, did he?"

"He did not say as much, *señor*. If he is such a thief as he is painted, undoubtedly he would merely have taken a horse without asking, had he wanted it."

"Ha! What business had he with you, then? It would be well for you to answer openly, *fray*!"

"Did I say that he had business with me?"

"Ha! By the saints—"

"The saints are better off your lips, *señor*—boaster and drunkard!"

"Do you wish to receive another beating, *fray*? I am riding on his excellency's business. Do not you delay me further! What said this pretty highwayman?"

"Nothing that I am at liberty to repeat to you, *señor*," Fray Felipe said.

Sergeant Gonzales pushed him aside roughly and entered the living-room, and his two troopers followed at his heels.

"Light the *candelero!*" Gonzales commanded his men. "Take candles, if you can find any. We search the house!"

"You search my poor house?" Fray Felipe cried. "And what do you expect to find?" Fray Felipe asked.

"I expect to find the piece of merchandise this pretty Señor Zorro left here, *fray*."

"What do you imagine he left?"

"Ha! A package of clothing, I suppose! A bundle of loot! A bottle of wine! A saddle to be mended! What would the fellow leave, *fray*? One thing impresses me—Señor Zorro's horse carried double when he arrived at your house, and was carrying none but Señor Zorro when he departed."

"And you expect to find—"

"The other half of the horse's load," replied Gonzales. "Failing to find it, we may try a twist or two of your arm to see whether you can be made to speak."

"You would dare? You would so affront a *fray*? You would descend to torture?"

"Meal mush and goat's milk!" quoth Sergeant Gonzales. "You fooled me once in some manner, but you will not so fool me again. Search the house, troopers, and be sure that you search it well! I shall remain in this room and keep this entertaining *fray* company. I shall endeavor to discover what his sensations were while he was being whipped for swindling."

"Coward and brute!" Fray Felipe thundered. "There may come a day when persecution shall cease."

"Meal mush and goat's milk!"

"When this disorder shall end and honest men be given their just dues!" Fray Felipe cried. "When those who have founded a rich empire here shall receive the true fruits of their labor and daring instead of having them stolen by dishonest politicians and men who stand in their favor!"

"Goat's milk and meal mush, *fray*!"

"When there shall be a thousand Señor Zorros, and more if necessary, to ride up and down El Camino Real and punish those who do wrong! Sometimes I would that I were not a *fray*, that I might play such a game myself!"

"We'd run you down in short order and stretch a rope with your weight," Sergeant Gonzales told him. "Did you help his excellency's soldiers more, perhaps his excellency would treat you with more consideration."

"I give aid to no spawn of the devil!" Fray Felipe said.

"Ha! Now you grow angry, and that is against your principles! Is it not the part of a robed *fray* to receive what comes his way and give thanks for it, no matter how much it chokes him? Answer me that, angry one!"

"You have about as much knowledge of a Franciscans' principles and duties as has the horse you ride!"

"I ride a wise horse, a noble animal. He comes when I call and gallops when I command. Do not deride him until you ride him. Ha! An excellent jest!"

"Imbecile!"

"Meal mush and goat's milk!" said Sergeant Gonzales.

THE BLOOD OF THE PULIDOS

The two troopers came back into the room. They had searched the house well, they reported, invading every corner of it, and no trace had been found of any person other than Fray Felipe's native servants, all of whom were too terrified to utter a falsehood, and had said they had seen nobody around the place who did not belong there.

"Ha! Hidden away well, no doubt," Gonzales said. "*Fray*, what is that in the corner of the room?"

"Bales of hides," Fray Felipe replied.

"I have been noticing it from time to time. The dealer from San Gabriel must have been right when he said the hides he purchased of you were not properly cured. Are those?"

"I think you will find them so."

"Then why did they move?" Sergeant Gonzales asked. "Three times I saw the corner of a bale move. Soldiers, search there!"

Fray Felipe sprang to his feet.

"Enough of this nonsense!" he cried. "You have searched and found nothing. Search the barns next, and then go! At least let me be master in my own house. You have disturbed my rest enough as it is."

"You will take a solemn oath, *fray*, that there is nothing alive behind those bales of hides?"

Fray Felipe hesitated, and Sergeant Gonzales grinned.

"Not ready to forswear yourself, eh?" the sergeant asked. "I had a thougt you would hesitate at that, my robed Franciscan! Soldiers, search the bales!"

The two men started toward the corner. But they had not covered one-half the distance when Señorita Lolita Pulido stood up behind the bales of hides and faced them.

"Ha! Unearthed at last!" Gonzales cried. "Here is the package Señor Zorro left in the *fray's* keeping! And a pretty package it is! Back to *carcel* she goes! And this escape will but make her final sentence the greater!"

But there was Pulido blood in the *señorita's* veins, and Gonzales had not taken that into account. Now the *señorita* stepped to the end of the pile of hides, so that light from the *candelero* struck full upon her.

"One moment, *señores!*" she said.

One hand came from behind her back, and in it she held a long, keen knife such as sheep skinners used. She put the point of the knife against her breast, and regarded them bravely.

"Señorita Lolita Pulido does not return to the foul *carcel* now or at any time, *señores!*" she said. "Rather would she plunge this knife into her heart, and so die as a woman of good blood should! If his excellency wishes for a dead prisoner, he may have one!"

Sergeant Gonzales uttered an exclamation of annoyance. He did not doubt that the *señorita* would do as she had threatened, if the men made an attempt to seize her. And while he might have ordered the attempt in the case of an ordinary prisoner, he did not feel sure that the governor would say he had done right if he ordered it now. After all, Señorita Pulido was the daughter of a don, and her self-inflicted death might cause trouble for his excellency. It might prove the spark to the powder magazine.

"*Señorita*, the person who takes his or her own life risks eternal damnation," the sergeant said. "Ask this *fray* if it is not so. You are only under arrest, not convicted and sentenced. If you are innocent, no doubt you soon will be set at liberty."

"It is not time for lying speeches, *señor*," the girl replied. "I realize the circumstances only too well. I have said that I will not return to *carcel*, and I meant it—and mean it now. One step toward me, and I take my own life!"

"*Señorita*—" Fray Felipe began.

"It is useless for you to attempt to prevent me, good *fray*," she interrupted. "I have pride left me, thank the saints! His excellency gets only my dead body, if he gets me at all."

"Here is a pretty mess!" Sergeant Gonzales exclaimed. "I suppose there is nothing for us to do except retire and leave the *señorita* to her freedom!"

"Ah, no, *señor*!" she cried quickly. "You are clever, but not clever enough by far. You would retire and continue to have your men surround the house? You would watch for an opportunity, and then seize me?"

Gonzales growled low in his throat, for that had been his intention, and the girl had read it.

"I shall be the one to leave," she said. "Walk backward, and stand against the wall, *señores!* Do it immediately, or I plunge this knife into my bosom!"

They could do nothing except obey. The soldiers looked to the sergeant for instructions, and the sergeant was afraid to risk the *señorita's* death, knowing it would call down upon his head the wrath of the governor, who would say that he had bungled.

Perhaps, after all, it would be better to let the girl leave the house. She might be captured afterward, for surely a girl could not escape the troopers.

She watched them closely as she darted across the room to the door. The knife was still held at her breast.

"Fray Felipe, you wish to go with me?" she asked. "You may be punished if you remain."

"Yet I must remain, *señorita*. I could not run away. May the saints protect you!"

She faced Gonzales and the soldiers once more.

"I am going through this door," she said. "You will remain in this room. There are troopers outside, of course, and they will try to stop me. I shall tell them that I have your permission to leave. If they call and ask you, you are to say that it is so."

"And if I do not?"

"Then I use the knife, *señor!*"

She opened the door, turned her head for an instant and glanced out.

"I trust that your horse is an excellent one, *señor*, for I intend to use it," she told the sergeant.

She darted suddenly through the door, and slammed it shut behind her.

"After her!" Gonzales cried. "I looked into her eyes! She will not use the knife—she fears it!"

He hurled himself across the room, the two soldiers with him. But Fray Felipe had been passive long enough. He went into action now. He did not stop to consider the consequences. He threw out one leg, and tripped Sergeant Gonzales. The two troopers crashed into him, and all went to the floor in a tangle.

Fray Felipe had gained some time for her, and it had been enough. For the *señorita* had rushed to the horse and had jumped into the saddle. She could ride like a native. Her tiny feet did not reach halfway to the sergeant's stirrups, but she thought nothing of that.

She wheeled the horse's head, kicked at his sides as a trooper rushed around the corner of the house. A pistol ball whistled past her head. She bent lower over the horse's neck, and rode!

Now a cursing Sergeant Gonzales was on the veranda, shouting for his men to get to horse and follow her. The tricky moon was behind a bank of clouds again. They could not tell the direction the *señorita* was taking except by listening for the sounds of the horse's hoofs. And they had to stop to do that—and if they stopped they lost time and distance.

THE CLASH OF BLADES AGAIN

Señor Zorro stood like a statue in the native's hut, one hand grasping his horse's muzzle. The native crouched at his side.

Down the highway came the drumming of horses' hoofs. Then the pursuit swept by, the men calling to one another and cursing the darkness, and rushed down the valley.

Señor Zorro opened the door and glanced out, listened for a moment, and then led out his horse. He tendered the native a coin.

"Not from you, *señor*," the native said.

"Take it. You have need of it and I have not," the highwayman said.

He vaulted into the saddle and turned his horse up the steep slope of the hill behind the hut. The animal made little noise as it climbed to the summit. Señor Zorro descended into the depression on the other side, and came to a narrow trail, and along this he rode at a slow gallop, stopping his mount now and then to listen for sounds of other horsemen who might be abroad.

He rode toward Reina de Los Angeles, but he appeared to be in no hurry about arriving at the *pueblo*. Señor Zorro had another adventure planned for this night, and it had to be accomplished at a certain time and under certain conditions.

It was two hours later when he came to the crest of the hill above the town. He sat quietly in the saddle for some time, regarding the scene. The moonlight was fitful now, but now and then he could make out the plaza.

He saw no troopers, heard nothing of them, decided that they had ridden back in pursuit of him, and that those who had been sent in pursuit of Don Carlos and the Doña Catalina had not yet returned. In the tavern, there were lights, and in the *presidio*, and in the house where his excellency was a guest.

Señor Zorro waited until it was dark, and then urged his horse forward slowly, but off the main highway. He circled the *pueblo*, and in time approached the *presidio* from the rear.

He dismounted now, and led his horse, going forward slowly, often stopping to listen, for this was a very ticklish business and might end in disaster if a mistake were made.

He stopped the horse behind the *presidio*, where the wall of the building would cast a shadow if the moon came from behind the clouds again, and went forward cautiously, following the wall as he had done on that other night.

When he came to the office window, he peered inside. Captain Ramón was there, alone, looking over some reports spread on the table before him, evidently awaiting the return of his men.

Señor Zorro crept to the corner of the building, and found there was no guard. He had guessed and hoped that the *comandante* had sent every available man to the chase, but he knew that he would have to act quickly, for some of the troopers might return.

He slipped through the door and crossed the big lounging-room, and so came to the door of the office. His pistol was in his hand, and could a man have seen behind the mask, he would have observed that Señor Zorro's lips were crushed in a thin straight line of determination.

As upon that other night, Captain Ramón whirled around in his chair when he heard the door open behind him, and once more he saw the eyes of Señor Zorro glittering through his mask, saw the muzzle of the pistol menacing him.

"Not a move! Not a sound! It would give me pleasure to fill your body with hot lead!" Señor Zorro said. "You are alone—your silly troopers are chasing me where I am not."

"By the saints—" Captain Ramón breathed.

"Not so much as a whisper, *señor*, if you hope to live. Turn your back to me!"

"You would murder me?"

"I am not that sort, *comandante!* And I said for you to make not a sound! Put your hands behind your back, for I am going to bind your wrists!"

Captain Ramón complied. Señor Zorro stepped forward swiftly, and bound the wrists with his own sash, which he tore from his waist. Then he whirled Captain Ramón around so that he faced him.

"Where is his excellency?" he asked.

"At Don Juan Estados's house."

"I knew as much, but wanted to see whether you prefer to speak the truth to-night. It is well if you do so. We are going to call upon the governor."

"To call—"

"Upon his excellency, I said. And do not speak again! Come with me!"

He grasped Captain Ramón by the arm and hurried him from the office, across the lounging-room, out of the door. He piloted him around the building to where the horse was waiting.

"Mount!" he commanded. "I shall sit behind you, with the muzzle of this pistol at the base of your brain. Make no mistake, *comandante*, unless you are tired of life. I am a determined man this night."

Captain Ramón had observed it. He mounted as he was directed, and the highwayman mounted behind him, and held the reins with one hand and the pistol with the other. Captain Ramón could feel the touch of cold steel at the back of his head.

Señor Zorro guided his horse with his knees instead of with the reins. He urged the beast down the slope, and circled the town once more, keeping away from the beaten trails, and so approached the rear of the house where his excellency was a guest.

Here was the difficult part of the adventure. He wanted to get Captain Ramón before the governor, to talk to both of them, and to do it without having anybody else interfere. He forced the captain to dismount, and led him to the rear wall of the house. There was a *patio* there, and they entered it.

It appeared that Señor Zorro knew the interior of the house well. He entered it through a servant's room, taking Captain Ramón with him, and passed through into a hall without awakening the sleeping native. They went along the hall slowly. From one room came the sound of snoring. From beneath the door of another light streamed.

Señor Zorro stopped before that door and applied an eye to the crack at the side of it. If Captain Ramón harbored thoughts of voicing an alarm, or of offering battle, the touch of the pistol at the back of his head caused him to forget them.

And he had scant time to think of a way out of this predicament, for suddenly Señor Zorro threw open the door, hurled Captain Ramón through it, followed himself, and shut the door quickly behind him. In the room, there were his excellency and his host.

"Silence, and do not move!" Señor Zorro said. "The slightest alarm, and I put a pistol ball through the governor's head! That is understood? Very well, *señores!*"

"Señor Zorro!" the governor gasped.

"The same, your excellency. I ask you, host to be not frightened for I mean him no harm if he sits quietly until I am done. Captain Ramón, kindly sit across the table from the governor. I am delighted to find the head of the state awake and awaiting news from those who are chasing me. His brain will be clear, and he can understand better what is said."

"What means this outrage?" the governor exclaimed. "Captain Ramón, how comes this? Seize this man! You are an officer—"

"Do not blame the *comandante,*" Señor Zorro said. "He knows it is death to make a move. There is a little matter that needs explanation, and since I cannot come to you in broad day as a man should, I am forced to adopt this method. Make yourselves comfortable, *señores.* This may take some little time."

His excellency fidgeted in his chair.

"You have this day insulted a family of good blood, your excellency," Señor Zorro went on. "You have forgotten the proprieties to such an extent that you have ordered thrown into your miserable *carcel* a *hidalgo* and his gentle wife and innocent daughter. You have taken such means to gratify a spite—"

"They are traitors!" his excellency said.

"What have they done of treason?"

"You are an outlaw with a price put upon your head. They have been guilty of harboring you, giving you aid."

"Where got you this information?"

"Captain Ramón has an abundance of evidence."

"Ha! The *comandante*, eh? We shall see about that! Captain Ramón is present, and we can get at the truth. May I ask the nature of your evidence?"

"You were at the Pulido *hacienda*," the governor said."

"I admit it."

"A native saw you, and carried word to the *presidio*. The soldiers hurried out to effect your capture."

"A moment. Who said a native sounded the alarm?"

"Captain Ramon assured me so."

"Here is the first chance for the captain to speak the truth. As a matter of fact, *comandante*, was it not Don Carlos Pulido himself who sent the native? The truth!"

"It was a native brought word."

"And he did not tell your sergeant that Don Carlos had sent him? Did he not say that Don Carlos had slipped him the information in whispers while he was carrying his fainting wife to her room? Is it not the truth that Don Carlos did his best to hold me at his *hacienda* until the soldiers arrived, that I might be captured? Did not Don Carlos thus try to show his loyalty to the governor?"

"By the saints, Ramón, you never told me as much!" his excellency cried.

"They are traitors!" the captain declared stubbornly.

"What other evidence?" Señor Zorro asked.

"Why, when the soldiers arrived, you concealed yourself by some trick," the governor said. "And presently Captain Ramón himself reached the scene, and while he was there you crept from a closet, ran him through treacherously from behind, and made your escape. It is an evident fact that Don Carlos had hidden you in the closet."

"By the saints!" Señor Zorro swore. "I had thought, Captain Ramón, that you were man enough to admit defeat, though I knew you for a scoundrel in other things. Tell the truth!"

"That is—the truth!"

"Tell the truth!" Señor Zorro commanded, stepping closer to him and bringing up the pistol. "I came from that closet and spoke to you. I gave you time to draw blade and get on guard. We fenced for fully ten minutes, did we not?

"I admit freely that for a moment you puzzled me, and then I solved your method of giving battle and knew you were at my mercy. And then, when I could have slain you easily, I but scratched your shoulder. Is not that the truth? Answer, as you hope to live!"

Captain Ramón licked his dry lips, and could not meet the governor's eyes.

"Answer!" Señor Zorro thundered.

"It is—the truth!" the captain acknowledged.

"Ha! So I ran you through from behind eh? It is an insult to my blade to have it enter your body! You see, your excellency, what manner of man you have for *comandante* here! Is there more evidence?"

"There is!" the governor said. "When the Pulidos were guests at the house of Don Diego Vega, and Don Diego was away, Captain Ramón went to pay his respects, and found you there alone with the *señorita.*"

"And that shows what?"

"That you are in league with the Pulidos! That they harbored you even in the house of Don Diego, a loyal man. And when the captain discovered you there, the *señorita* flung herself upon him and held him—delayed him, rather—until you made your escape through a window. Is not that enough?"

Señor Zorro bent forward, and his eyes seemed to burn through the mask and into those of Captain Ramón.

"So that is the tale he told, eh?" the highwayman said. "As a matter of fact, Captain Ramón is enamored of the *señorita*. He went to the house, found her alone, forced his attentions upon her, even told her that she should not object, since her father was in the bad graces of the governor! He attempted to caress her, and she called for help. I responded."

"How did you happen to be there?"

"I do not care to answer that, but I take my oath the *señorita* did not know of my presence. She called for aid, and I responded.

"I made this thing you call a *comandante* kneel before her and apologize. And then I took him to the door and kicked him out into the dust! And afterward I visited him at the *presidio*, and told him that he had given insult to a noble *señorita*—"

"It appears that you hold some love for her yourself," the governor said.

"I do, your excellency, and am proud to admit it!"

"Ha! You condemn her and her parents by that statement! You deny now they are in league with you?"

"I do. Her parents do not know of our love!"

"This *señorita* is scarcely conventional!"

"*Señor!* Governor or no, another thought like that and I spill your blood!" Señor Zorro cried. "I have told you what happened that night at the house of Don Diego Vega. Captain Ramón will testify that what I have said is the exact truth. Is it not, *comandante?* Answer!"

"It—it is the truth!" the captain gulped, looking at the muzzle of the highwayman's pistol.

"Then you have told me falsehood, and can no longer be an officer of mine!" the governor cried. "It appears that this highwayman can do as he pleases with you! Ha! But I still believe that Don Carlos Pulido is a traitor, and the members of his family, and it has availed you nothing, Señor Zorro, to play this little scene.

"My soldiers shall continue to pursue them—and you! And before they are done, I'll have the Pulidos dragged in the dirt, and I'll have you stretching a rope with your carcass!"

"Quite a bold speech!" observed Señor Zorro. "You set your soldiers a pretty task, your excellency. I rescued your three prisoners to-night, and they have escaped."

"They shall be retaken!"

"Time alone will tell that. And now I have another duty to perform here! Your excellency, you will take your chair to that far corner, and sit there, and your host will sit beside you. And there you shall remain until I have finished."

"What do you mean to do?"

"Obey me!" Señor Zorro cried. "I have scant time for argument, even with a governor."

He watched while the two chairs were placed and the governor and his host had seated themselves. And then he stepped nearer Captain Ramón.

"You insulted a pure and innocent girl, *comandante*!" he said. "For that, you shall fight! Your scratched shoulder is healed now, and you wear your blade by your side! Such a man as you is not fit to breathe God's pure air! The country is better for your absence! On your feet, *señor*, and on guard!"

Captain Ramón was white with rage. He knew that he was ruined. He had been forced to confess that he had lied. He had heard the governor remove his rank. And this man before him had been the cause of all of it!

Perhaps, in his anger, he could kill this Señor Zorro, stretch this Curse of Capistrano on the floor with his life blood flowing away. Perhaps, if he did that, his excellency would relent.

He sprang from his chair, and backward to the governor.

"Unfasten my wrists!" he cried. "Let me at this dog!"

"You were as good as dead before—you certainly are dead after using that word!" Señor Zorro said calmly.

The *commandante's* wrists were untied. He whipped out his blade, sprang forward with a cry, and launched himself in a furious attack upon the highwayman.

Señor Zorro gave ground before this onslaught, and so obtained a position where the light from the *candelero* did not bother his eyes. He was skilled with a blade, and had fenced for life many times, and he knew the danger in the attack of an angered man who did not fence according to the code.

And he knew, too, that such anger is spent quickly unless a fortunate thrust makes the possessor of it victor almost at once. And so he retreated step by step, guarding well, parrying vicious strokes, alert for an unexpected move.

The governor and his host were sitting in their corner, but bending forward and watching the combat.

"Run him through, Ramón, and I reinstate and promote you!" his excellency cried.

The *comandante* thus was urged to do it. Señor Zorro found his opponent fighting much better than he had before in Don Carlos Pulido's house at the *hacienda*. He found himself forced to fight out of a dangerous corner, and the pistol he held in his left hand to intimidate the governor and his host bothered him.

And suddenly he tossed it to the table, and then swung around so that neither of the two men could dart from a corner and get it without running the chance of receiving a blade between the ribs. And there he stood his ground and fought.

Captain Ramón could not force him to give way now. His blade seemed to be a score. It darted in and out, trying to find a resting place in the captain's body; for Señor Zorro was eager to have an end of this and be gone. He knew that the dawn was not far away, and he feared that some trooper might come to the house with a report for the governor.

"Fight, insulter of girls!" he cried. "Fight, man who tells a falsehood to injure a noble family! Fight, coward and poltroon! Now death stares you in the face, and soon you'll be claimed! Ha! I almost had you then! Fight, cur!"

Captain Ramón cursed and charged, but Señor Zorro received him and drove him back, and so held his position. The perspiration was standing out on the captain's forehead in great globules. His breath was coming heavily from between his parted lips. His eyes were bright and bulging.

"Fight, weakling!" the highwayman taunted him. "This time I am not attacking from behind! If you have prayers to say, say them—for your time grows short!"

The ringing blades, the shifting feet on the floor, the heavy breathing of the combatants and of the two spectators of this life-and-death struggle were the only sounds in the room. His excellency sat far forward on his chair, his hands gripping the edges of it so that his knuckles were white.

"Kill me this highwayman!" he shrieked. "Use your good skill, Ramón! At him!"

Captain Ramón rushed again, calling into play his last bit of strength, fencing with what skill he could command. His arms were as lead; his breath was fast. He thrust, he lunged—and made a mistake of a fraction of an inch!

Like the tongue of a serpent, Señor Zorro's blade shot in. Thrice it darted forward, and upon the fair brow of Ramón, just between the eyes, there flamed suddenly a red, bloody letter Z!

"The Mark of Zorro!" the highwayman cried. "You wear it forever now, *comandante!*"

Señor Zorro's face became more stern. His blade shot in again and came out dripping red. The *comandante* gasped and slipped to the floor.

"You have slain him!" the governor cried. "You have taken his life, wretch!"

"Ha! I trust so! The thrust was through the heart, excellency! He never will insult a *señorita* again!"

Señor Zorro looked down at his fallen foe, regarded the governor a moment, then wiped his blade on the sash that had bound the *comandante's* wrists. He returned the blade to its scabbard, and picked up his pistol from the table.

"My night's work is done!" he said.

"And you shall hang for it!" his excellency cried.

"Perhaps—when you catch me!" replied the Curse of Capistrano, bowing ceremoniously.

Then, without glancing again at the twitching body of him who had been Captain Ramón, he whirled through the door and was in the hall and rushed through it to the patio and to his horse.